The Santa Fe Trail by Air
A Pilot's Guide to the Santa Fe Trail

William W. White

Published by
Western Airtrails
Logan, Utah

The Santa Fe Trail by Air
A Pilot's Guide to the Santa Fe Trail

By William W. White

Published by:
>   Western Airtrails
>   P.O. Box 6071
>   North Logan, Utah 84341

ISBN 0-9655085-0-1

51495

9 780965 508506

To the members of
The Santa Fe Trail Association
for their efforts in the preservation
of trail sites and the
Spirit of the Trail

All photographs by the author.

Cover Photo: Bent's Old Fort, LaJunta, Colorado

Table of Contents

Acknowledgment

My deepest thanks to:

The Santa Fe Trail Association for contributing to the preservation of Trail remnants that first caught my attention.

Marc Simmons whose writings inspired the research necessary for this book.

My sister Janet who spent hours laughing at and correcting my attempts to reinvent the English language and its rules of grammar and punctuation.

Nate Smith who spent hours in the darkroom trying to undo the effects of haze, motion and a non professional photographer.

And to all the folks that offered encouragement and help.

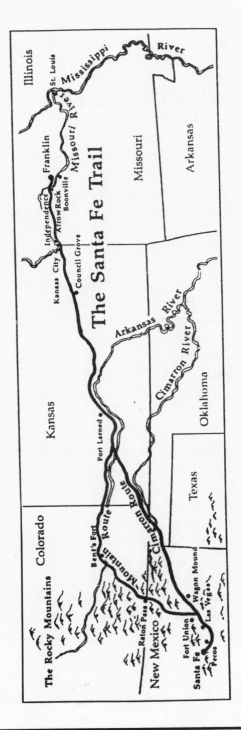

The Santa Fe Trail
Courtesy of National Park Service

Disclaimer

It saddens me to have to include this page in this book but in a world of litigation the choice is not mine.

This guide is intended to be used as an aid for planning only and is not intended to be or to replace current navigation planning publications! The reproductions of segments of the sectional charts <u>are not to scale</u> and <u>should not be used for navigation</u>. Distances and bearings are approximate and should not be used for calculations that involve the safety of your flight. Fuel stops become more widely spaced as you fly west, so always fly on the top half of your tanks.

Every effort has been made to provide accurate information as of the time of printing. Because time changes all, the information may not be correct by the time that you read this book. Please use the telephone to verify information prior to your departure.

The cautions that are listed on the waypoint pages are not intended to be complete listings of the cautions necessary for a safe flight. Common sense and judgment of individual pilots are beyond our control and we can assume no responsibility for the lack of either.

Density altitude <u>will</u> become a factor along the route so become familiar with the effects of thin air on your aircraft's performance before you depart. Instruction or experience in mountain flying is <u>strongly</u> recommended.

If the above remarks are not insulting enough to your intelligence, read on. The following clause is mandatory. Please accept my apology.

If you do not want to be bound by the above, return this book to the publisher for a full refund.

Preface

Soon after I purchased my 182 in 1992, I began to suffer the effects of "buyer's remorse." The thrill of the freedom to travel began to be replaced by the questions of "Where?" and "Why?" As I pursued the quest for adventure, the $100 hamburger soon began to escalate in price. In spite of rising cholesterol levels and a swelling waistline, I felt unfulfilled as I paid for the fuel that my 182 had burned while helping me kill time and destroy my health. Realizing that burnout was just around the corner, I thought "There has to be something to do with my plane that will provide something besides heartburn."

On a flight from Santa Fe, New Mexico, to Ennis, Montana, I chose a route that would take me north along the eastern edge of the Colorado Rockies. I had planned to fly over an area near Laramie, Wyoming, where on a previous flight I had spotted a group of rock rings that I had been told were "tipi rings." After departing Santa Fe on my way to see these rings that were supposedly used to hold down the edges of Indian tents, I passed over the airport at Las Vegas, New Mexico. (Yes, there is another Las Vegas!) At the southern end of the main runway I noticed some strange markings on the ground and began to circle the area. As I expanded my point of view, I noticed that the marks formed lines that led to the northeast. Not long after I started to follow the strange lineal markings a light came on between my headphones. "Whoa! Those are ruts made a hundred and fifty years ago by wagons on the Santa Fe Trail." I continued to follow the ruts for 45 minutes and soon realized that I had found an alternative to the expensive burger.

After returning to my home in Utah, I began to research the history of the Santa Fe Trail. The fascination quickly spread to the other western trails. Countless hours of research enabled me to plot the course of the Santa Fe Trail on sectional charts. With the next break in the weather, I anxiously departed Utah for Gardner, Kansas, to begin tracking the Trail to the "City Different," as Santa Fe is also known. As the historical landmarks I had read about came into view ahead of my 182, I experienced something that I can only express as "almost spiritual." At that point, I decided to write this guide so that others might experience the thrill of following the route to Santa Fe and gain some insight into what life must have been like on the Trail, traveling almost eight hundred miles across hostile countryside to a foreign territory and the promise of riches.

Detailed descriptions of life on the frontier provided some of the most interesting information I discovered while researching this guide. I compiled some of that information into a brief fictional diary. It is nowhere near all-inclusive, but the journal will give you an idea of what life was like along the route to Santa Fe in the mid 1800s. The sequence and dates are fictional but the details and concepts are accurate depictions that have been gleaned from the journals of those who traveled the Trail. If you allow your imagination to run wild as you read the journal, the trip along the route will have a greater impact and increase your sense of appreciation for the hardships endured by the early traders.

The Santa Fe Trail by Air is intended to be used as an aid to help you plot and plan a trip that will be an informative and educational alternative to "the burger." It is not intended to be a comprehensive history of the Trail—hundreds of books have already covered the subject extensively.

INTRODUCTION

Fort Union near Las Vegas, New Mexico

Introduction

The Santa Fe Trail by Air was designed to aid pilots who plan to use either their pilotage skills or a GPS/Loran to plot and fly the Santa Fe Trail. This guide must in no way be used as a substitute for a well-planned flight. The use of **current** sectionals and airport information is vital to a safe air tour. For the most part, the flight avoids restricted and congested airspace. However, the route closely approaches several restricted areas, Class D airspaces, MOAs and numerous uncontrolled airports. AIM procedures for proper radio notification should be followed.

While searching for ruts and other landmarks, it is very easy for the pilot's concentration to be diverted from the necessities of safe flight. Special care must be given to maintaining safe ground clearances while in a turn searching for ground references. For this reason, I suggest an extra margin of safety be considered. Many of the features that you will be trying to locate are actually **easier to see** at 1500 feet AGL or higher. Low level flight may position you close to the traffic patterns of the numerous airports along the route as well as some rather high radio towers.

Those pilots venturing into the mountainous terrain of the West for the first time would be well advised to take a mountain flying course before leaving home. Airports are more widely spaced in the western states, so careful planning for fuel, food, and relief will make the trip more pleasant. The prevailing winds will be from the west (headwinds) so do not stretch your fuel reserves. Mountain waves, turbulence, sudden afternoon thunderstorms and microbursts make morning flight the preferred choice. I suggest that you fly early, when the light is better for photography, and then spend a leisurely afternoon at one of the ground attractions listed in the Appendix.

A few moments taken now to familiarize yourself with this guide will save time later. The guide is divided into four sections. The first section is introductory information about planning to fly the Santa Fe Trail. The next section is a brief history of the Santa Fe Trail and a fictional Trail journal from the summer of 1845 to provide you with background information for your adventure. The third section is the detailed information you will need to plot the Trail, a list of waypoints and the route description. The last section is the Appendix that includes miscellaneous information to help you plan your trip. You will notice some repetition from one section to another—there is a reason. This guide is designed to be read once for general information, but it is assumed the reader will need time to assemble materials and current sectionals and will be doing the actual plotting at another time, and then at a later date make reservations and do final planning. So, some information has been repeated to jog the reader's memory since the history and journal will probably not be read each time.

Read the section on "Plotting the Trail" and then glance over the list of waypoints, near the center of this book, and notice the different column headings. The "**Waypoint ID**" column lists the suggested designator for GPS usage and for marking the charts as you plot the route. Using the suggested designator will simplify the process of following the route description and sidebars that accompany the photographs. The "**Waypoint Name**" column is either the city or town shown on the sectionals, a location name used in the journals or an arbitrary name used to identify the waypoint. The "**Sectional**" column indicates which chart to use; "**N**" or "**S**" indicates which side of the chart to use. The "**Latitude**" and "**Longitude**" columns list the degrees and minutes of each waypoint location. The "**Bearing to Next**" and "**Range to Next**" columns list the *magnetic heading* and the distance (to the nearest mile) in *nautical miles* to the next waypoint. The reason for these listings will become obvious as you begin to plot the route. The information in the waypoint list is identical to the information listed on each page of the route description section.

The main body of the guide is the route description section. Each page contains the waypoint information (described above) and a reproduction of a section of the appropriate chart with the approximate route of the Trail marked by a bold black line. **Remember, these maps are not to scale and should not be used for navigation.** The depicted route is meant to be used as an aid in plotting the route on **current** sectionals, from the waypoint listed at the top of the page to the next waypoint. "**Special Cautions**" are listed under the waypoint information when deemed advisable. "**Days on the Trail**" indicates the approximate number of days the wagons would have been on the Trail after they left the Gardner area in 1845.

The page opposite each map contains a photo of the waypoint to enable you to visually verify your position and to help you accurately locate the less obvious features. These photos were taken from various altitudes and may not depict the exact view that you will have from your plane. For the most part they show the view from an east to west direction of travel. The photographs are not intended to be works of art—their function is to help you locate waypoints.

The Appendix contains information that will be useful in the final stages of the planning process. FBO information, local phone numbers of rental car agencies and lodging facilities at the listed airports are noted under the name of the closest town. The evaluations are subjective and are based on the way I was treated before the providers knew that I was researching this guide. Special mention is given to FBOs with courtesy cars and motels that offer airport pickup. Ground attractions are listed with their hours of operation, seasons and fees. If time permits, contact the chamber of commerce for the listed town. The information that they offer will be very valuable in the planning process.

The Santa Fe Trail actually begins at Franklin, Missouri, forty-some miles east of the first waypoint. Because of the crowded airspace around Kansas City and the lack of features visible from the air in that area, this guide begins west of there at Gardner, Kansas, where the Santa Fe Trail and the Oregon Trail split and go in separate directions. There are several books in print, designed for motorists, which list many more sites along the Trail than does this guide. Since many of those landmarks are monuments and highway markers not easily visible from the air, they have not been included in this guide. In some cases, the waypoint locations are not exactly over the ground reference listed but are offset to enhance the view from the air.

The route that is described in this guide is reasonably accurate. If you are a stickler for detail, I suggest obtaining the National Park Service book *Santa Fe National Historic Trail* or Gregory Franzwa's *Maps of the Santa Fe Trail* from your local library. These publications contain extremely detailed maps of the entire Trail.

If your trip is meant to be an educational experience for adults or children, I suggest that you explore some of the other reading materials listed in the Appendix **before you fly** the Trail. Seeing the ruts and landmarks will have a much greater impact if one can attach some meaning to the sightings.

Good luck on your flight. I hope it will be as meaningful for you as it is for me each time that I fly it.

As this book is going to print, Western Airtrails is in the final stages of preparing a similar guide to the Oregon, California and Mormon Trails. If you ordered this guide by phone or mail, you will be notified by newsletter when the next guide becomes available. If you purchased this guide from a retail outlet, call us or drop us a line and we will include you on our customer list. This mailing list **will not be sold or shared**, so your inquiry will not lead to a flood of junk mail.

If you have any comments or questions about *The Santa Fe Trail by Air*, or if you discover new features along the Trail, please let us know. All suggestions about this or our other guides are truly welcomed. Thanks for your support.

Western Airtrails
1-888-755-0330
P.O. Box 6071
North Logan, Utah 84341

Suggested Itinerary

Day 1—
Arrange to fly the section of the Trail from Gardner (SF01) to Fort Larned (SF09) early in the morning. Plan to spend the night in Great Bend or Larned and visit the Santa Fe Trail Center and Fort Larned.
Approximate mileage: 200 nm

Day 2—
Fly from SF09 to SF13 early in the morning and then head for La Junta (LHX) and Bent's Old Fort (SFM3). Find the ruts at Willow Bar so you will know where to pick up the Trail the next morning. The approximate heading to LHX is 337° and the range is 98 nm. Along the way to LHX, watch for ruts that mark the many versions and cutoffs of the Trail and later stagecoach and military roads. The afternoon will disappear quickly if you visit Bent's Old Fort. Take comfortable walking shoes, plenty of film and a picnic lunch.
Approximate mileage: 300 nm

Day 3—
Depart LHX and return to Willow Bar (SF13). Relocate the ruts that lead to the southwest. Follow the route at a slow pace and watch for ruts that parallel the main route all the way to Las Vegas, New Mexico. If ground transportation is a problem at Las Vegas, continue to Santa Fe.
Approximate mileage: 280 to 320 nm

Day 4—
Fly or drive from Santa Fe to Las Vegas and visit Fort Union and the historic area of downtown Las Vegas. A nice side trip is to visit Philmont Scout Ranch and then continue to Cimarron, New Mexico. The return trip to Las Vegas or Santa Fe can be made on the interstate.

The Ruts

Spotting wagon ruts from the air will undoubtedly be one of the highlights of the trip. In many places modern roads follow the route of the Trail and some of the guide books will refer to the dirt roads as "ruts." In this guide, only sections of the Trail that are not overrun with modern tracks will be referred to as "ruts." Although some ruts are obvious, locating and identifying many of the ruts requires a keen eye and a basic understanding of how they were formed.

From the air the Trail may appear as a single pair of ruts or a number of parallel swales. Along the eastern portion of the route most of the original track has been destroyed by agricultural activity, road construction or other man-made efforts at progress. Nature has taken a toll in some places, while in other places the effects of erosion have actually contributed to the enhancement and preservation of the ruts. The dry desert area from Willow Bar to Las Vegas, New Mexico, has preserved the ruts so well that they will provide you with the most accurate means of navigation along the route.

A few moments spent reflecting upon human nature and the travel conditions in the 1840s will make spotting the few surviving ruts much easier. Think "Where would I go if I were driving a wagon through here?" Your intuition is perhaps the most valuable tool for locating the scars of the wagons' wheels. For example, watch for straight lines that do not normally occur in nature. (If the line or track is *too* straight, it is probably a pipeline or other utility easement.) Tracks that look like old dirt roads, but seem to start nowhere and seem to go nowhere, are likely candidates. Spotting ruts from the air is an art, not a science, and as in all arts, practice enhances the skill.

The passing of hundreds of wagon wheels altered the soil characteristics enough that the vegetation in some of the tracks will be visibly different from the surrounding flora. Where the Trail made a steep ascent or descent in the more arid areas, erosion may have blended the wheel tracks into a single wide wash or *arroyo*. Ruts that were formed from east to west often have been deepened by the prevailing westerly winds, while those running north to south often have been drifted closed and lost forever by the same winds.

Using "the best tool," imagine being behind several hundred wagons rolling along through dust that was reported to be ankle deep. Moving to the side would be prudent at the least. This parallel tracking resulted in ruts that could be miles to the side of the "trail." Grass was the "gasoline" of the wagon trains and as more and more trains used the Trail each year, it was often necessary to move several miles to the side of the beaten path to find an area that had not been grazed to bare ground. Some of these ruts are visible today and provide a challenge to the observant pilot/crew. The multiple ruts are most visible between Wagon Mound and the Las Vegas airport.

Fort Union and Fort Larned provide opportunities to actually walk in sections of the ruts. Since many of the other ruts that you will see from the air are on private property, flying the Trail provides a perspective that is unattainable to those bound by gravity. If walking in the ruts is of interest to you, contact the Santa Fe Trail Association. They sponsor periodic outings that offer rare opportunities to walk in the ruts across lengthy sections of the Trail. This privately-funded organization has made tremendous progress in its attempts to preserve sections of the Trail. The association's address is listed in the Appendix. Visit the Santa Fe Trail Center if you stop at Larned.

If you are bitten by the "Trail bug" and want to pursue a more detailed understanding of the Trail's history, a list of additional reading is included in the Appendix.

Using GPS Along the Trail

During the research for this guide, I used a Garmin 55 AVD GPS. The programming instructions that you are about to read are based on my experience with this incredible little gadget. The details may vary from brand to brand but the principles are the same. Please verify the programming instructions in your owner's manual.

Flying point to point using a GPS will cause you to miss much of the Trail. But using a GPS to verify waypoints or to return to a waypoint will really enhance the trip, especially after circling a section of ruts or another ground feature. Using the "Range to Next" feature will enable you to recognize many of the waypoints as you approach them. If your GPS offers a choice of range scales, select nautical miles so the range mileage will more closely match those on the waypoint list.

For the Santa Fe Trail, your GPS will need to have room for 26 user waypoints. How you build your routes will depend on how you plan to fly the Trail. Using the designators on the waypoint list (SF01, SFM1, etc.), enter the latitude and longitude for all the waypoints according to your GPS manufacturer's instructions. A word to the wise—if your GPS has a navigation planning feature use it to verify the "Bearing to Next" and "Range to Next" listed on the waypoint list. If there is a discrepancy of more than a degree or two, or of more than a couple of miles, take the time to verify that the entered latitude and longitude match those on the list **exactly.** A transposed number entered in either the latitude or longitude can lead to a frustrating and potentially dangerous side trip. **Take the time to verify the data before you try to fly the Trail, and always verify your position with the charts.**

Remember, bearing and range information is line of sight. Use the GPS for verification only. **DO NOT** use the listed ranges for flight planning.

THE SANTA FE TRAIL

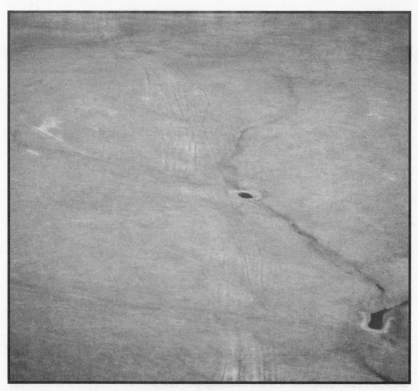

Ruts west of Point of Rocks, New Mexico

A Brief History of the Santa Fe Trail

There are many wonderful books that deal with the history of the Santa Fe Trail in great detail. (Some of these books are listed in the Appendix at the end of this guide.) During the research phase of this guide, it became clear that any attempt to create a comprehensive history of the Santa Fe Trail would be beyond the scope of this book. The following is a very brief accounting of the events that led to the development of the Trail and of its colorful history.

The beginning of Trail history preceded the landing of the Pilgrims at Plymouth Rock. By 1540, the Spanish explorer Coronado had traveled across the southwestern region of what was to become the United States. In his search for gold, Coronado roamed as far east as present day Wichita, and the Spanish began to claim as theirs the lands of the Southwest. As the search for gold continued, missionaries began a quest to save the souls of the Indians. In the 1600s Spanish colonization efforts continued throughout the Southwest and gradually began to alarm the Indians of the area. By 1680, the Indian people had had enough and drove the Spaniards from the region. The Indians' reclamation lasted until 1692 when Diego de Vargas restored Spanish rule to New Mexico.

About the same time, the French were beginning to explore the Gulf Coast and the Mississippi River basin. As the race for territorial claims escalated, the Spanish began an expansion to the east and the west. This led to a conflict of territorial boundaries that was settled in 1763 when the French agreed to give the Spaniards the Louisiana Territory. In 1800 a secret treaty returned the territory to French rule. When Napoleon sold the territory to President Thomas Jefferson in 1803, the United States instantly became a neighboring threat to the Spanish claims to the Southwest. The actual boundaries of this land acquisition were vague at best until a treaty between Spain and the United States established a firm definition of the territory boundaries in 1819.

After 250 years of occupation, the Spanish were well established in what is now the New Mexico area. Santa Fe was a city about to celebrate its 200th anniversary. Any growing city requires a steady supply of goods and supplies to sustain its growth and Santa Fe was no exception. From the time the city was founded, supplies had to be shipped almost a thousand miles from central

Mexico. All trade was controlled by the Spanish government and the merchants of Santa Fe were prohibited from buying from other than Spanish-controlled sources. This trade restriction led to grossly inflated prices and pent-up demand.

The stage was set for the inevitable. In 1821 the political factor of Spanish isolationism was eliminated when Mexico gained independence from Spanish rule. The geographical factor of isolation was diminishing as the United States boundary became contiguous to the Mexican territory. As U.S. settlers moved westward, the dwindling distance to the lucrative Santa Fe market put substantial financial gain within reach of profit-seeking traders. On September 1, 1821, a young trader named William Becknell left the American frontier with several pack animals bound for the untried market of Santa Fe. When he arrived on November 16, Becknell's goods were immediately sold for a huge profit (2000%). After his return to Franklin, Missouri, Becknell bragged about his profits and reported that wagons could make the trip. The reaction to his news was immediate. Before Becknell could organize another expedition, others had already left—driving wagons loaded with trade goods.

The ruts leading to Santa Fe were rapidly being deepened by 1824 when wagon trains with hundreds of wagons headed to Santa Fe. In 1825, just four years after Becknell's first trip, the government allocated $30,000 for a survey of the Trail. Even in the 1800s some thought this a waste of money since one only had to follow the well-worn ruts to instant wealth. By now the trip to Santa Fe had become an adventure which attracted tourists. Young people flocked to the wagon trains, hoping to be hired as teamsters. (Among these was a 16-year-old lad named Kit Carson who had run away from home.) If you remember the Alaska pipeline project in the 1970s, you will see that some things don't change much.

Unlike the adventurers who went to Alaska, those who traveled the Santa Fe Trail had to deal with hostile Indians. By 1829, the traders were requesting military protection. Because of the value of the Santa Fe market, soldiers began escorting traders to the Mexican border (which at that time was the Arkansas River) where Mexican forces assumed the role of escorting the wagons to their destination. The wagons enjoyed the protection of the Mexican troops as they returned to the border where the U.S. forces awaited their return. Tourism increased as the Trail became safer and commercial enterprises began to sprout up along the route. In 1833 Bent's Old Fort was established at the border along the Arkansas River to supply the travelers. Soon Mexican merchants began to travel to the "States" to buy goods to haul back to their own territory. At that time the Mexicans claimed most of the Southwest from what we know as central Oregon south, western Colorado, and all of Texas.

In 1836 Texas won independence from Mexico and became a sovereign republic. By 1840, the Texans were raiding Mexican trade caravans and U.S. trade goods were being hauled into the interior of Mexico. When the Mexicans realized the threat that foreign trade could be to their economy, they imposed a $500 tax on each wagon entering their territory. "Yankee ingenuity" responded by manufacturing and using huge wagons that hauled much larger loads than the standard wagons. When the Texas Republic joined the Union in 1845, the Mexicans had had enough of the U.S. Doctrine of Manifest Destiny.

The Mexican War broke out in 1846 as the Mexicans defended their territory against U.S. expansion. Most of the warfare was concentrated in southern Texas but required that huge wagon trains encroach on Mexican lands to supply the military. The Doctrine of Manifest Destiny was not restricted to southwestern expansion. The first major wagon trains were leaving the Missouri River banks headed for California (also a Mexican possession) and the Oregon Territory (recently seceded by the British). As the war continued through 1847, the Mormons were heading to the Salt Lake Valley (also in Mexican territory). The boundaries of Mexico's land claims proved to be too large to defend. The Treaty of Guadalupe Hildago was signed in 1848 and the boundaries of the U.S. land claims in the Southwest became almost what they are today.

After the treaty was signed, it became necessary for the United States government to protect the new land claims. The military began to establish forts along the Trail to protect the huge quantities of supplies that were being transported to the new territory and to the forts themselves. The Indians were becoming more hostile toward the waves of intrusion. In one year, more than 300 wagons were destroyed, 6000 animals were stolen or killed, and nearly 50 people were killed. More military protection was needed, and more supplies were needed to feed the troops. The dollar value of goods moving across the Trail grew rapidly as the more affluent traders became involved. Goods were imported from Europe and shipped to the trailhead by railroad and steamship. In 25 years, Becknell's little venture had evolved into a multimillion-dollar market.

When gold was discovered in California in 1849, traffic on the Trail skyrocketed as many took the southern route to the gold-fields. Fort Union was established in 1851 to protect the western end of the route. U.S. expansion continued westward as survey parties began to determine the routing for the coming railroads.

Salt Lake City was already well established and the British had relinquished their claim to the Northwest. California was in the midst of the gold rush and being settled at the rate of several hundred people a day. Trade flourished as American and Mexican wagon trains hauled thousands of tons of goods to the ever thirsty markets of the Southwest. Mail service was established and it became possible to send a letter from Santa Fe to St. Louis in two weeks and to receive a reply two weeks later. With the discovery of gold in Colorado in 1858, the volume of traffic on the Trail surged again to more than three million dollars that year alone. That volume tripled the next year as thousands of wagons deepened the ruts of the Trail.

By the time the Civil War broke out, the Trail was the 19th-century equivalent of an interstate highway. Most caravans used the Mountain Route to avoid conflict with the Confederate troops that were active in Texas. The effect of the war on the Trail and Santa Fe was minimal. Southern troops advanced from Texas to Pigeon Ranch (an undesignated landmark just south of waypoint SF20) where they had a brief skirmish with Union forces that had moved south from Colorado to protect the territory. The Confederates were actually gaining an edge over the Northerners when some "Yankees" slipped behind the line and destroyed the Confederate supply wagons. Without supplies, the Rebels were forced to retreat to Texas. Little sign of the Civil War remains along the Trail except at Fort Union where the distinct star-shaped earthen fortification is clearly visible from the air. The war had little effect on the volume of goods being hauled across the Trail but provided a force of trained fighters that the government utilized when the Indians became the new "target" of the military.

After the war, traffic on the Trail was heavy, but the end was near. The railroads were headed west. Ten years after the end of the war the Atchison, Topeka & Santa Fe had reached Pueblo, Colorado. All that was needed now was to extend the rails south past Santa Fe and on to California. Competition between railroads for the route was fierce and a court battle resulted in the right of way over Raton Pass being granted to the Atchison, Topeka & Santa Fe. The tracks eventually passed 18 miles south of Santa Fe, so passengers and freight still had to be hauled to town by wagon. Years later a branch linked the city to the main track at the small town of Lamy.

After a colorful and exciting history, the Santa Fe Trail was relinquished to a place in history. Commercially the Trail may have died, but to the many who have fought to preserve the landmarks, ruts and history, the Trail is alive and well.

As development and time continue to erode the physical remains, hopefully the spirit of the Trail will ride with you in the cockpit as you fly over the route. In ten or so years, more of the ruts will have worn away forever. But if the spirit stays with you, the efforts of this writing will be rewarded.

Life Along the Trail

To get the most out of your trip, it is necessary to use your imagination—try to visualize what the traders experienced and endured on a daily basis. In doing so, keep in mind that the conditions along the Trail should be compared first to the trials of everyday life during the first half of the 19th century and then to the lifestyles that we enjoy today. By our standards, even the "good life" in the 1800s appears harsh and trying. To best stimulate your imagination, allow yourself to travel along with the traders in the following fictional journal. The sequence is fictional, but the details and conditions are documented in the journals of the early merchants.

May 15 to June 10, 1845
Banks of the Missouri River near Independence, Missouri

Preparations for the trip are underway. For a successful commercial venture, the first step is to acquire the goods to be traded at the end of the Trail for gold and silver coins—the real motivation for the adventure. Some of the traders are buying knives, pots and pans, fabrics, and whiskey locally at prices that will allow a healthy profit. Serious traders have arranged for tons of goods to be shipped from Europe or the East coast by steamship or rail. The largest of the traders have lobbied for legislation that allows the government to refund import duties (levied on imported goods) when the goods leave Missouri bound for Santa Fe. The potential profits are large enough that competition is of small concern.

With the merchandise purchased and boxed, it is time to arrange the details of transportation. The wagons have been purchased from local sources or ordered from a major manufacturer like Studebaker. Since the Mexican government has levied a $500 tax on each wagon entering their country, profits can be maximized by using larger wagons capable of hauling more goods. Several manufacturers have designed huge wagons, with wheels seven feet in diameter, capable of carrying several tons of goods. These megawagons require more draft animals than the smaller wagons but the lesser tax per ton will increase the profits. The next step is to buy or rent the animals to pull the wagons to a market almost eight hundred miles away.

The traders on their first trip to New Mexico are buying high-priced horses because they are quicker and therefore will deliver the goods earlier than the slower wagons that are pulled by oxen. The more experienced traders are trying to make their best deals on mules because they have proven to be more durable than horses and faster than oxen. The "old-timers" are buying 5- to 7-year-old oxen. Harness makers are reaping windfall profits from those not wise enough to have had their tack shipped to the edge of the frontier. The old adage "it costs money to be poor" is once again proving to be true.

With the wagons and draft animals secured, it is time to hire the manpower that will drive the teams, hunt for fresh meat, and provide protection from Indians and bandits who are beginning to harass the caravans as they travel beyond the borders of the United States. The thrill of adventure has drawn hundreds of experienced teamsters and hundreds of inexperienced "greenhorns." The larger trading companies pay higher wages and hire the seasoned men. Selecting the right "crew" is a difficult situation. The men who are seeking adventure are an independent lot and not particularly fond of taking orders: military veterans, criminals, thrill seekers and "blowhards" are mixed in the pool of applicants. Wages average $20 per month and the men are responsible for feeding themselves. Working hours are several hours before daylight to well into the night, seven days a week for almost two months.

The job description is simple: "What ever in the hell is needed." The lives of the merchants who travel with their wagons will be in the hands of the men that they hire for $20 a month—a scary thought indeed!

June 11, 1845
Lone Elm Campground—Just west of the River

On the morning of departure, the atmosphere in camp approaches that of a circus as inexperienced men and animals try to establish an orderly rhythm that they will follow in the days to come. After several hours of chaos, the wagons line up and follow the well-established track toward the west. The ground is flat and the "road" well worn. Although women and children do travel the Trail, we have only men—and some boys about to become men—in our group.

When evening approaches, the wagons pull to the side of the track and camp takes shape. Some of the men gather wood for the fires and others tend to the animals. As the sun sets, a faint drone is heard at the edge of the trees. Within minutes some of the men begin to cough and curse as millions of mosquitoes descend on the camp in search of their evening meal. The men abandon their attempts to prepare the evening meal and they rush for the tents. They swat at the swarms of insects, realizing that they are the lucky ones—the men who are riding watch on the stock animals do not have an option to escape. When the black clouds of mosquitoes turn their attention to the helpless animals, the job of the herdsmen becomes more difficult as the animals react to the biting insects by trying to run away. Throughout the night the riders are kept busy trying to keep the animals from stampeding. The exhausted men swat at the mosquitoes until their hands are sore and their faces red with the blood of crushed insects.

June 12, 1845
East of "The Narrows"

Several hours before sunrise the mosquitoes return to the bushes and the day begins for the teamsters. As the stock animals are fitted with harness, a few men gather wood for the fires and others begin to cook breakfast. The tents are struck as the sun rises and soon the wagons begin to roll.

Conversations about the mosquitoes become exaggerated as the air warms. The relief of warming air excites more than the teamsters—hoards of "green flies" begin to swarm around the ears and necks of the animals. The annoyance of the mosquitoes is soon dwarfed by the voracious appetites of the horseflies. Teamsters curse and scream as the animals thrash against their harnesses, trying to escape the blood-sucking insects.

As suddenly as they appeared, the horseflies disappear when the sun fades behind ominously dark storm clouds. The wind begins to blow in earnest and a light rain bounces off the wagon covers. The noise is comforting at first. The road begins to turn to mud and the steel-tired wheels sink into the soft ground. The comforting sound of soft rain is replaced by the deafening roar of hail rebounding from wagon covers and the backs of man and beast. Sharp cracks of thunder make the animals nervous and as the intensity increases the men scream at the horses and oxen which try to run in fear, still attached to the wagons that are sinking deeper into the mud.

With the wagons buried in mud to the axles, the animals continue to panic. Harness traces are broken and some animals run toward the horizon dragging chains and pieces of the wagon rigging. Riders are dispatched to recover the stampeding animals, desperately trying to control their own mounts as they slip and slide in the mud. By now, all are soaked to the skin and shivering from cold. The storm continues throughout the afternoon.

The clouds finally begin to clear and the temperature drops as the day comes to an end. The animals that have not run off are herded into a circle formed with the wagons to serve as a temporary corral. Peacefulness settles over the camp as the men look forward to a cold night sleeping on wet ground in wet blankets. The evening meal consists of some dried fruit and stale crackers because any fuel is far too wet to burn. At the end of the second day of their trip, a few men begin to question the wisdom of their $20-a-month job. The seasoned veterans go to sleep mumbling, "I've seen worse!"

June 19, 1845
Council Grove

The eastern sky lightens with the rising sun, signaling the start of another day on the Trail. We have left several letters in a hole in an old oak tree that is called "Post Office Oak." We're hoping someone will carry them east and deposit them in a proper postal office. In turn, we have gathered letters bound for Santa Fe and will deliver them to the city when we arrive. After a hot breakfast of bacon, biscuits and coffee, the men's spirits begin to rise. A clear morning sky promises a good day of travel and we will try to make up for yesterday's losses. The road, although still soft, supports the wheels, and the horseflies are nowhere to be found. Only three horses were lost during the night and we decide to go on rather than to spend time looking for them.

The sun climbs higher in the clear blue sky, and the temperature rises at about the same rate. By the time the men stop for "nooning," a fine dust is churned into the air with each wagon wheel that passes over what was mud only hours ago. In spite of the heat, the wagons continue westward toward the next camping area that offers water and wood. The noon meal begins to cause cramps in several men—some of the bacon had gone bad. Sweat-drenched outer clothing is shed. The men stricken with food poisoning deal with their intestinal problems without benefit of facilities; the others continue to perspire and suffer the effects of the heat. Very little water is carried on the wagons because the campgrounds are next to streams and the weight-carrying capacity of the wagons has been reserved for profitable cargo. The parched teamsters are relieved when a soft breeze begins to blow and their sweat-soaked clothing provides a cooling effect, although too late for one man who collapses from heat exhaustion.

The wind increases as we approach the next camping area. After the first two nights, wind is a minor inconvenience. The tents are erected, our blankets have dried during the day, firewood is dry and plentiful, and the clear spring satisfies the thirst of animals and men. The traders dine on a meal of beans and rice followed by dried fruit that has been hauled from Missouri. The teamsters are roasting prairie dogs and sharing an antelope that one of the hunters shot earlier in the morning. (As part of their employment contract, the working men agreed to supply their own food.) With the approaching darkness the guards settle into the routine of keeping the animals from straying into the night.

After a quiet night, it is discovered that ten mules disappeared during the night. A tracker determines that a band of Indians had stolen the animals under the cover of darkness, in spite of an agreement between the government and the Indians. (In 1825 the government had paid the Indians $800 in goods to ensure safe passage of travelers through the territory.) The apparent breach of this treaty angers the traders and they decide to pursue the thieves in an attempt to recover the stolen animals. Ten heavily armed men leave camp following the tracks of the shod mules. Several hours later the animals are located in a dry stream bed and recovered.

As the search party returns to camp, a small band of Indians approaches the riders. The teamsters begin to curse the "thieving red devils." One of the men is overcome with anger and shoots one of the Indians off his horse. The remaining two Indians try to flee, but the teamsters kill them both with bullets to the back. The rescuers are heralded as heroes when they return to camp. *(Unfortunately, a single Indian observed the slaughter from the edge of a stand of trees. This group of traders will be gone by the time the observer reports back to the rest of his hunting party. The trigger-happy whitemen have no idea of the impact of their indiscretions. The next caravan, however, will be attacked by the entire hunting party as vengeance is sought by the Indians for the wanton slaughter of their comrades. Events like this led to the massive Indian Wars that occurred in the late 1800s.)*

June 27, 1845
Two days from the Little Arkansas Crossing

Our group resumes their travels toward the west and it promises to be a splendid day on the prairie. The sun is bright and the road is solid and well marked. Under these ideal conditions the wagons approach their target rate of travel—2 miles in an hour or 16 to 20 miles a day. During the noon stop several of the wagons require repair. It seems that in the dry prairie air the wood in the wheels has dried and shrunk, leaving the steel tires loose on the wheels. The wealthier traders have a blacksmith in the crew and a forge is set up to refit the tires. The poorer traders have to settle for jamming wooden wedges between the rims and the wheels. Trees had been cut from hardwood stands before leaving Missouri and the logs were slung under the wagons to provide a source of material if wagon tongues or axles needed to be replaced along the trail. Valuable space in the wagons is occupied by spare wagon parts, tools, and harness parts to repair almost any problem that occurs along the route.

June 29, 1845
Little Arkansas Crossing

After achieving our goal of 20 miles for the day, we stop along a small stream that promises good water and grass for the stock. Since it's an early stop, the teamsters take advantage of the opportunity to deal with "housekeeping" chores. Those deciding to bathe jump into the stream before the cooks prepare the evening meal. As the men wash off the grime from a week on the dusty trail, the cooks gather the water for coffee just *downstream* from the bathers. Ample firewood is gathered from the stream bank, allowing the cooks to bake bread in the Dutch ovens. The aroma of a good meal fills the air for the first time in several days. The men begin to relax with their bellies full and the crud from the trail washed away. A feeling of renewal comes over several of the teamsters. This is the first day in a week that they had not been plagued with severe intestinal disturbances which in turn created problems with the forward movement of the caravan because the men had to stop several times an hour to relieve their distress along the road. This slowed the entire caravan since the wagons behind also had to stop and wait. All rejoiced in the prospect of a better day tomorrow.

June 30, 1845
East of Plum Buttes

At sunrise one of the men is missing, but he is soon found along the stream curled up in the fetal position complaining of stomach pains. *(Unknown to the caravan, another wagon train had camped upstream several days earlier while they waited for several men to die of cholera. The microscopic organisms from the dying men had been washed into the stream and were consumed with a drink of water by the now screaming teamster.)* It becomes apparent to the leaders of the train that the dreaded cholera has stricken our caravan. The symptoms are obvious. Uncontrollable diarrhea and vomiting are caused by inflammation of the bowel. The men retreat to the rear of the camp to make plans for the burial because they know death will occur within a few hours. The symptoms of cholera appear rapidly. Soon the man is so dehydrated that the skin on his fingers begins to sag and his eyes appear sunken as his body loses water at the rate of a liter an hour. A deep hole is dug in the middle of the trail as the rest of the teamsters await the end. After the death, the body is wrapped in a saddle blanket and placed in the hole. A layer of rocks is piled on the body and the hole is then filled in to ground level. The wagons begin to move westward again, making sure to drive over the fresh grave with their wheels. To the green-horns this appears barbaric but the seasoned teamsters know that this is the most effective way to hide the grave from the prying eyes of the Indians who have been watching the train for several days from a distance of a mile or so. With the grave camouflaged, perhaps the Indians will not dig up the grave to strip the body of clothes, and maybe the wolves will not smell the body and dig up the easy meal.

Just yesterday we passed a grave that had been exhumed by Indians. The body had been butchered and mutilated beyond description. The teamsters thought it more prudent to leave the area as soon as possible rather than take the time to rebury the remains. It is clear that the Indians are beginning to perceive the white intruders as enemies rather than curiosities as they did originally. An old-timer related that the mutilation of an enemy's body assures that the body and the spirit will not be reunited—the ultimate destruction of an enemy. Each tribe of Indians has a unique method of mutilation, so the experienced teamsters are able to identify the hostiles from the type of carnage to the corpse. Tonight the men watching the livestock will not have a problem staying awake. Sign of hostile Indians puts the whole caravan on their guard

To the greenhorns **all** Indians are a threat and the "only good Indian is a dead Indian" attitude permeates the men. The same small group of natives that has been following the train for several days is still visible on the horizon. The younger men want to ride out and kill them and it is all the old-timers can do to keep order in the ranks. As the caravan winds its way west, the Indians begin to approach the wagons. Orders are given to "hold your fire." Two of the natives ride to the wagon under a white flag and the lead merchants begin to communicate with them through an old trapper who has been riding with the wagons. It appears that the Indians only want to trade furs with the traders. The older and wiser men decide it is better to appease the two rather than to become hostile. Soon the transaction is completed and the Indians ride back to their awaiting comrades.

Early in the afternoon one of the younger men spots an antelope passing behind the caravan, and with visions of fresh meat, he rides the backtrack to do a little hunting. Three miles down the road his absence is noticed and several riders are dispatched to find the strayed greenhorn. Two hours and three miles later the riders return with the man's body tied across a saddle. The telltale mutilation of his body indicates that the "friendly" Indians, who had been in camp only hours before, had spotted the straying whiteman, killed him and stolen his mount. Tonight the guard will be doubled and few will sleep.

July 5, 1845
Below Pawnee Rock

While we set up camp for the night, the old-timers explained why their choice for draft animals had been oxen. First, the Indians have little need for cattle because they cannot ride them into battle like they can the stolen horses and mules. Second, the oxen move so slowly that they are hard to steal, whereas the horses and mules can be driven out of rifle range quickly. Third, as an old and slow ox's throat was cut, they explained that the oxen provide a convenient source of fresh meat.

As the ox bones were picked clean under the stars, several men became extremely ill from overindulging in the first fresh meat in more than a week. Several hours later, one of the younger men began to suffer from violent chills. His symptoms are all too familiar to the old-timers, but with no doctor available within hundreds of miles, the poor lad will have to suffer with the often fatal effects of malaria. Riding in the back of a bouncing wagon, he will probably be dead within three days. By now burials are becoming rather common. Measles killed two men the day before yesterday.

July 9, 1845
At the Arkansas River Crossing

The more experienced traders are glad they have the resources to hire extra men, while the less well-funded merchants are wondering if they will have enough manpower to get all their wagons to Santa Fe. In an attempt to restore their previous levels of manpower, the smaller traders send several men westward along the Arkansas River to Bent's Fort with hopes of recruiting additional men for the balance of the trip. Soon we will cross to the south bank of the river and in doing so will leave U.S. territory and enter the land of a foreign country. The most serious and dangerous part of the journey is yet to come. Reports of massive Indian attacks had filtered back to Missouri before we left and we know that the *Jornada*, a waterless stretch of desert, has to be crossed before reaching Santa Fe. Plans are made to rest the animals and the men for several days before the crossing.

July 13, 1845
On the banks of the Arkansas River

The riders have returned from Bent's Fort with several new recruits and we cross the Arkansas River *(near what will become Cimarron, Kansas)*. Since we left Missouri we have been following one river or another. This is not a coincidence—the riverbeds are relatively flat and for the most part are aligned with the direction of travel. The hundreds of animals require huge quantities of water and the rivers have satisfied that need for most of the way so far. We have been told that this convenience is about to change as we head southwest toward the Cimarron River that will lead us toward Santa Fe and our anticipated profits. Every conceivable container is filled with water and the firearms are made ready for instant use.

The most noticeable change in the landscape is in the grass. The lush grasses of the riverbeds have been replaced by wiry prairie grasses. Firewood is scarce and becoming scarcer with the passing of each caravan.

Less than three miles from the Arkansas the trail turns to a dusty track where the dry particles of soil have the texture of flour and flow with the consistency of water around the spokes of the wheels. With the passing of each wagon, the dust is churned into the air until the last wagons disappear in the clouds of alkali. Mucus in the noses and throats of the men and animals turns to mud as they gasp for air. When the dust becomes unbearable, the wagons begin to leave the track and seek a dust-free route parallel to the established track. The caravans that follow will also spread out laterally and deepen the paralleling tracks. *(Many of these parallel tracks will endure for more than a century.)* Part of the churned-up soil blows away in the wind and the dust that remains turns to mud with the first drops of rain. As the rain intensifies, we watch the fragile desert soil wash toward the oceans leaving deep scars that turn to slippery mud within minutes.

July 14, 1845
On the *Jornada*

Today the animals and men approached a state of exhaustion and the leaders established a camp near a water hole that has the appearance of a swampy marsh. The animals have had nothing to drink since leaving the river and several wagons were damaged as the animals stampeded toward the smell of the water. The experienced teamsters unhitched their wagons a mile before the water hole to avoid having their wagons destroyed by runaway animals. As the animals quenched their thirsts and began to graze on the sparse grasses that surround the small oasis, the men dug holes in the mud to collect what water was left to quench their own thirsts.

Kettles of the muddy liquid were placed over the fire and heated to kill the "wigglers" (insect larvae). The wigglers died in the boiling water and sank to the bottom of the containers. While the water was still warm, the men gulped it down to replenish the fluids lost through perspiration during the 80° day. (*Thousands of amoeba, protozoa and bacteria are ingested with each gulp. Giardiasis, amebic dysentery, coli, salmonella and shigellosis will take a toll in the days to come, adding to the stress on human systems that are already taxed by the heat and the waterless desert. The men were "lucky" today as this water hole contained no typhoid fever bacteria.*)

There was no wood or even brush to fuel the cooking fires so a few men set off in search of buffalo "chips." Being dispatched to gather the prairie's alternative fuel was enough to humble several rough and tumble teamsters. Buffalo feces consists of partially digested grass that burns very clean but very fast. Gathering three and a half bushels of "chips" for each cooking fire soon became the job of the greenhorns. (*This precious fuel will become more scarce as the buffalo population declines because of the wanton slaughter by the white intruders.*)

July 15, 1845
Lower Spring of the Cimarron River

Huge herds of buffalo have been seen in the distance for the last several days. Today the hunters got lucky and several of the teamsters rode off to help retrieve the meat. Six cows were killed and the hunters returned with the humps, tongues, choice cuts of meat from the hind quarters and the intestines. A feast was enjoyed by all. The tongue and humps were roasted over the fire, but the real treat was the intestine which was baked with the contents intact. This bizarre source of vegetable matter turned the stomachs of the greenhorns. The rest of the meat was left to the coyotes and wolves. (*Years later some of these same traders would complain about the declining herds of buffalo, unable to relate the killing of the breeding cows with that decline. The Indians, who had relied on the huge animals for centuries to provide food, fuel and hides, also noticed the declining herds and quickly established the correct cause and effect relationship. The irritation and anger caused by the increasing presence of the whitemen began to be replaced with a desperate sense of survival. Conflict between the Native Americans and the whitemen would increase for decades to come.*)

July 17, 1845
Middle Spring of the Cimarron River

It has been a dry year and as our train approaches the next campground we notice that the spring at the edge of the now dry Cimarron River has also dried up. Shovels are unpacked and several shallow wells are dug. Subterranean water fills the holes and is hauled to the animals who are becoming weaker by the day because of poor grazing and lack of water. The horses are the first to fall. The old-timers again explain their choice of oxen because of the bovines' ability to survive conditions that kill horses and mules. More than half a dozen animals have died in the traces since the wagons left the Arkansas River. The spare animals that have been herded along behind the wagons now are called to serve in harness to replace those left to rot along the side of the trail. The stench of decaying animal flesh fills the air except when the wind blows hard from the west.

We headed out of camp. The land is flat and dry with not a tree in sight. The weather has been warm but a slight breeze from the west made traveling almost pleasant. In mid afternoon dark clouds appeared on the northwest horizon. As the sky darkened, the wagon covers began to flap in the increasing wind. Soon the covers started to tear and the loose ends snapping in the wind sounded like rifle fire. Dust obliterated the trail ahead and the animals began to show signs of panic. During the struggle to control the stock, one of the old-timers screamed a curse as he pointed to the northwest. A huge funnel-shaped cloud was only miles away. With no shelter for men or beast, the men tried to tie the wagons together in an attempt to keep them upright.

All attempts to control the stock were abandoned as the men ran for their lives and fought for the scant shelter afforded by the small bushes in an *arroyo* (a dry stream bed). Ten minutes later a calm settled over the scene. Only one wagon had been destroyed and its contents were scattered over several acres. More than a hundred oxen and mules had stampeded, running off in all directions. A few horses were recaptured and the men began to gather the other animals. A camp was established here because the leaders know that regrouping the caravan will take several days.

July 18, 1845
Still at Middle Spring

This unfortunate disaster could not have happened at a worse place along the Trail. The Comanche Indians are a particularly violent tribe and have killed many whitemen on the desert section of the route. (*Contrary to popular belief, the Indians rarely attacked the wagons en mass. It was far more likely that bands of natives would shadow the caravans for weeks, just out of rifle range, and wait for a straggler to fall behind or a small group of hunters to venture beyond the protective cover of the caravan.*) This is why many of the smaller trading parties waited at the banks of the Arkansas River for other small parties and then formed large caravans of a hundred wagons or more. Safety in numbers was a lesson learned early in the history of the Trail. Now with so many of the men scattered in all directions trying to gather the stock, the caravan is more vulnerable than at any time since we left Missouri.

July 19, 1845
Still in camp

Not only are our lives at risk but the rich bounty in the wagons is becoming a tempting target for the Indians. The saving grace turns out to be that the Indians are more interested in the horses and mules than the trade goods. Several years ago the opposite would have been true but as the hostilities have increased, the advantages of being mounted on a horse have taken priority over obtaining the traditional beads and trinkets used for trading in earlier years. (*During several years of the Trail's history, livestock losses would amount to thousands of horses and mules.*) Today, with many of the men scattered in small groups, there is little hope of recovering all the stock animals. It will be a lucky day if all the men return unharmed.

The leaders know that several times in the past weeks when "friendly" Indians have approached the wagons, there was a strong possibility that they were actually spies sent to evaluate the strength of our defenses. Rather than risk a confrontation, the leaders chose to allow the Indians to come and go in peace. The wisest of the merchants realize that many of the stories of Indian attacks are often exaggerated and that to react to those stories would only serve to guarantee more attacks before reaching Santa Fe.

(In these early years of the Trail, the Indians were more interested in stealing animals than killing the white intruders. Several years in the future, as the whitemen killed more buffalo and began to settle along the Trail, the Indian's motivations would change to a more defensive mode. Diseases that were introduced by the traders were killing hundreds of Indians. The Indians' established way of life on the plains was being threatened and they reacted like any other people who were faced with starvation and epidemics of disease. "Reacting" was not limited to the Indians. Often, truly friendly Indians would approach the wagons only to be slaughtered by inexperienced traders who had heard rumors of Indian massacres and reacted out of fear and ignorance.)

July 24, 1845
McNees Crossing

Around the breakfast fire an old trapper told us the story of McNees Crossing. Near here, in 1828, several hostile Indians had killed two white traders who had gone ahead of their wagons to scout the route. About the time the wagons came upon the bloody site, some truly friendly Indians rode up to meet the wagons—oblivious to the slaughter of the whitemen. As the Indians approached, the traders opened fire and killed all but one of the natives. The survivor returned to his encampment and related the story of the whites killing his comrades. As could be expected, the Indians rallied to extract revenge and the caravan lost many men and animals as the result of their "reacting" to the deaths of McNees and his companion. This is the type of calamity that the wiser traders tried to avoid.

(The Indians were masters of guerrilla and psychological warfare a century before the tactics of stealth and patience were to be named. Small bands of Indians often followed the wagons just out of rifle range or stampeded the animals in the middle of the night. They often howled like wolves, keeping the stock agitated and the men from sleeping. The grass that was so necessary for the survival of the animals was sometimes burned ahead of a caravan thus depriving the animals of food. Those unfortunate enough to be caught away from the wagons often were killed and their bodies mutilated. All these activities caused the stress levels in the men to rise. Truly masters at psychological warfare, the Indians gradually wore their victims down. As the men began to show the signs of stress, diseases took a greater toll and the rate of accidents increased. The Indians were patient—they had weeks before the wagons reached the safety of the troops at Fort Union (after 1851). As harassment by the Indians intensified, the Mountain Route became more popular because it avoided the territories of the Comanches and the Apaches.)

August 1, 1845
Canadian River

The dangerous days of the trip are growing fewer as we approach the Canadian River. After crossing this small river, Wagon Mound will come into view. The men need this psychological boost. The animals are weakening with each passing day. In this desert area the grass is poor when it is at its best and the water is drying up as the daytime temperatures approach 90°. Our caravan consists of 72 wagons. Each wagon is pulled by six to eight animals in harness. Combined with the 200+ animals being driven behind the wagons, the total number of animals needing to graze for several hours each day is over 750. That many animals eat a tremendous amount each day and it has been difficult to find areas which have not been grazed to the ground by the animals that pulled the hundreds of wagons preceding ours this year. It is often necessary to get several miles off the established trail to find grass for the stock.

It seems that the animals have an ability to smell water several miles before the wagons reach the springs or streams. Driven by their thirst, the animals that are not in harness explode in stampede as they rush toward the water. Many of our spare oxen actually arrived at the Canadian River several hours ahead of our wagons. Camp is made for the day on the banks of the river to let the animals rest before the push to Wagon Mound and the springs at its base.

August 3, 1845
Apache Spring – Wagon Mound

At breakfast, several of the men announce that they are no longer able to walk because their legs have become swollen and are bleeding under the skin. All of the affected men are from the smaller trading parties. The leader of the caravan recognizes the symptoms of scurvy. The wealthier traders have brought potatoes, onions and pickled cabbage along for their men, and their employees have been spared from the effects of the disease. The poorer traders' men have survived on meat and bread and are more susceptible to scurvy's devastating effects. Relief is only days away for the men. Fresh vegetables and fruit await the caravan at the small community where the Mountain Route of the trail rejoins the route that we are on. Wagon Mound is today's destination and a small party of men has been sent ahead to scout for Apaches that sometimes lay in ambush near the spring.

August 4, 1845
La Junta

Today, as we neared the junction, a small band of Mexicans met our wagons. Their pack horses were loaded with melons, squash, onions and green peppers. The men suffering from scurvy anxiously bought the produce and there was a feast of fresh food at the noon stop. The Mexicans advised the leaders to divert to the east because the grass was better near a small stream that could be followed tomorrow back to the main route. This evening, as the animals enjoyed the first *green* grass in two weeks, the men's spirits were lifted because of the fresh produce and the knowledge that our trip is nearly over. Santa Fe is only six days away.

August 6, 1845
San Miguel

Today when we approached the small town of San Miguel on the Pecos River the townspeople rode out to meet us, and it was noticed that many of the people had severely pockmarked faces. One of the old-timers told us that the scars were caused by smallpox and that those with the scars were the lucky ones. When the disease struck a population, the death rate was often more than 50%. *(This terrible disease was unknown to the native people until it was introduced by the whiteman. Whole villages were destroyed as smallpox spread through the indigenous populations who had no resistance to the disease.)* Many of the men, especially the ones employed by the wealthier merchants, were inoculated before leaving Missouri. Smallpox vaccine was developed in the 1700s but not all of the men had taken advantage of that protection. Men from the poorer wagons became nervous when they saw the graphic effects of the disease.

The residents of San Miguel hosted a celebration this evening. The men ate and danced until well into the night. The return to civilization—even this crude civilization—was cause to rejoice. Many will travel tomorrow with headaches from an evening of drinking and other overindulgence.

August 8, 1845
Pecos Mission

Tonight we camped near an ancient building which we were told was an old mission several hundred years ago. The structure is huge, built from the red earth and local stone. The day after tomorrow we will enter the city of Santa Fe.

August 10, 1845
Santa Fe

We arrived in Santa Fe late this afternoon and most of the men were paid and dismissed from their employ. A few will continue with several of the merchants who are bound for the interior of Mexico. For those men the trip is only half over. For those of us not going on, this first night in Santa Fe is something that we have been looking forward to since leaving Missouri. Whiskey and good times are easily procured and the night will be a long one. *(The party atmosphere of Santa Fe was responsible for the eventual relocation of the military personnel to Fort Union (in 1851) on the eastern flanks of the Sangre de Cristo Mountains. Drunken brawls and sexually transmitted disease were claiming more soldiers than did many battles with Mexico during the war.)*

We have traveled 753 miles since leaving Independence, Missouri. If we had chosen the Mountain Route, the distance would have been 797 miles. As long as the trip was, some of the merchants are planning to return to Missouri this fall. After selling many of their wagons and some of the livestock in the local market, there will be fewer wagons in the returning caravans. The merchants will group together near La Junta so that the caravans will be large enough to provide protection against Indian attacks. The wagons will be lightly loaded and the teamsters plan to make the trip in two-thirds of the time it took to travel to Santa Fe. Gold, silver, furs and Mexican blankets make a lighter load but provide a tempting target for marauders and thieves. As bad as the grass was on the trip west, it will be even worse later in the year on the return to the States.

I will spend the winter in Santa Fe and take the opportunity to rest and reflect upon the adventures of the summer past.

Bien Venidos.

FLYING THE SANTA FE TRAIL

Waypoint ID:	Waypoint Name:	Latitude:	Longitude:	Bearing to next:	Range to next:	Sectional:	N or S Side:
SF01	Gardner, KS	N 38° 49'	W 94° 58'	263°	33.7 nm	Kansas City	N
SF02	State Lake Ruts	N 38° 47'	W 95° 41'	254°	39.2 nm	Kansas City	N
SF03	Council Grove	N 38° 39'	W 96° 30'	255°	11.9 nm	Kansas City	N
SF04	Diamond Spring	N 38° 37'	W 96° 45'	250°	12.1 nm	Kansas City	N
SF05	Lost Spring	N 38° 34'	W 97° 00'	238°	13.2 nm	Wichita	N
SF06	Durham Ruts	N 38° 28'	W 97° 15'	247°	33.8 nm	Wichita	N
SF07	Little Arkansas Crossing	N 38° 18'	W 97° 56'	274°	22.4 nm	Wichita	N
SF08	Ralph's Ruts	N 38° 22'	W 98° 24'	248°	40.1 nm	Wichita	N
SF09	Fort Larned	N 38° 11'	W 99° 13'	240°	58.5 nm	Wichita	N
SF10	Cimarron, KS	N 37° 48'	W 100° 21'	236° to SF11	54.1 nm	Wichita	S
				285° to SFM1	26.5 nm		
SF11	Wagon Bed Spring	N 37° 24'	W 101° 22'	231°	52.3 nm	Wichita	S
SF12	Willow Bar	N 36° 57' ,	W 102° 18'	238°	40.2 nm	Wichita	S

Waypoint ID:	Waypoint Name:	Latitude:	Longitude:	Bearing to next:	Range to next:	Sectional:	N or S Side:
SF13	McNees Crossing	N 36° 41'	W 103° 04'	242°	27.3 nm	Wichita	S
SF14	Round Mountain	N 36° 32'	W 103° 36'	248°	26.5 nm	Wichita	S
SF15	Point of Rocks	N 36° 26'	W 104° 08'	236°	19.5 nm	Denver	S
SF16	Canadian River Crossing	N 36° 18'	W 104° 30'	202°	20.0 nm	Denver	S
SF17	Wagon Mound	N 36° 01'	W 104° 43'	215°	18.4 nm	Denver	S
SF18	Watrous, NM	N 35° 48'	W 104° 59'	209°	11.6 nm	Denver	S
SF19	Las Vegas Airport, NM	N 35° 39'	W 105° 08'	263°	40.0 nm	Albuquerque	N
SF20	Sante Fe, NM-City	N 35° 41'	W 105° 57'	None		Denver	S
SFM1	Garden City, KS	N 37° 58'	W 100° 52'	267°	89.6 nm	Wichita	N
SFM2	Bent's New Fort	N 38° 05'	W 102° 45'	256°	32.5 nm	Wichita	N
SFM3	Bent's Old Fort	N 38° 02'	W 103° 26'	213°	57.9 nm	Wichita	N
SFM4	Trinidad Ruts	N 37° 19'	W 104° 15'	204°	57.7 nm	Denver	S
SFM5	Cimarron, NM	N 36° 31'	W 104° 55'	174° to SF18	43.1 nm	Denver	S

Waypoint ID:	SF02
Waypoint Name:	State Lake Ruts
Sectional:	Kansas City-N
Latitude:	38° 47´ N
Longitude:	95° 41´ w
Next Waypoint:	SF03
Bearing to Next:	254°
Range to Next:	39.2 nm
Days on the Trail:	4

Cautions: Radio towers.

Route from SF02 to SF03

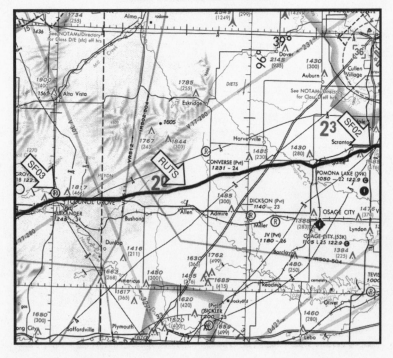

State Lake Ruts

The State Lake ruts are not significant or easy to see from the air. Do not spend too much time searching. The Trail continues west and passes through downtown Burlingame. There are several short sections of ruts scattered along the route on the way to Council Grove. The best are 2 miles north of Allen and parallel Rt. 56 (noted on the map).

In the days of the Trail, the trees that you see below you were not present. Periodic prairie fires killed the seedlings and small trees before they could gain a foothold. Man's efforts to suppress these natural, seasonal fires has changed the landscape.

Waypoint ID:	SF01
Waypoint Name:	Gardner, KS
Sectional:	Kansas City-N
Latitude:	38° 49′ N
Longitude:	94° 58′ W
Next Waypoint:	SF02
Bearing to Next:	263°
Range to Next:	33.7 nm
Days on the Trail:	0

Cautions: Two busy airports with controlled airspace (OJC and IXD) and uncontrolled K34 are at the edge of the veil of the Kansas City Class B airspace. The Trail junction is **DANGEROUSLY CLOSE** to (IXD) and (K34).

Route from SF01 to SF02

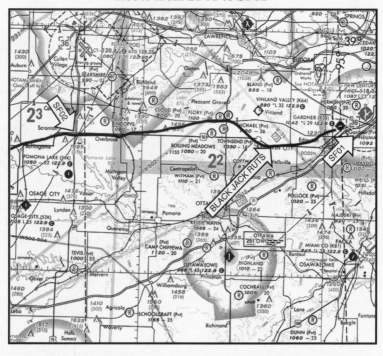

General area of the Santa Fe and Oregon Trail junction

There is not much to see here but since the Santa Fe Trail and the Oregon Trail split and go their separate ways at Gardner, it has been chosen as the starting point for this guide. The Santa Fe Trail, in use for 25 years before the Oregon Trail, was primarily a freight route, while the longer Oregon Trail was used for human migration.

As you pass over Baldwin City, you will be directly over the Trail. There is a short section of ruts 2 miles east of town and just south of Rt. 56. This section is labeled as the "Blackjack Ruts" on the map.

Plotting the Trail

To plot and fly the Santa Fe Trail you will need the following **current** sectionals:

- · Kansas City
- · Wichita
- · Denver
- · Albuquerque

Using sectionals rather than WAC charts will make plotting and flying the Trail much easier, and the features on the sectionals, such as CTAF and FSS frequencies, will make the flight safer. The plotting process will be more accurate if you use a see-through plotter with a protractor large enough to span two-thirds of the way across the space between the lines of latitude and longitude. Be sure to use **current** charts.

Before you begin to plot the Trail, **please** take the time to read the following instructions **completely**. If you do, the plotting process will be as simple as a child's game of connect the dots.

1. Begin with the waypoint list, the route description page for the first waypoint (SF01), and your Kansas City sectional opened to the North side.

2. By using the listed latitude and longitude for SF01 and referring to the small map on the route description page, find Gardner, just southwest of Kansas City. Got it? At that exact point make a mark that is large enough to be visible in the clutter on the chart, being careful not to cover any critical information (towers, etc.).

3. Now, using the information for SF02, locate and mark that waypoint. (Your mark should be at the north edge of the small three-fingered lake.)

4. Continue to plot SF03 and SF04 (both are on the Kansas City-N sectional).

5. Next, turn back to the route description page of SF01 and draw the route on the Kansas City-N sectional as it is shown on the small map, again being careful not to cover any critical information on the sectional. Continue the process for SF02, SF03, and SF04. See? Connect the dots!

That's all there is to it! Repeat the process for the remaining waypoints on the other three sectionals. The route that you have just drawn will be a reasonably accurate depiction of the route of the Santa Fe Trail.

After you have plotted the route, start at the first waypoint and **carefully** follow the route looking for and marking radio towers, special use airspace and airports along the route. (A highlighting marker works well for this.) If you are interested in the ruts, make notations on your sectional along the route (using a different color highlighting marker) where the small maps have ruts noted that are not waypoints. The color coding will make locating the ruts easier from the air.

Note: When you plot the Mountain Route between SFM3 and SFM4 there may be some confusion. The sectional charts do not fit together very well. There is a small section (four miles) of the Trail on the southeast corner of the Denver-N that will fill the missing gap. The Trail follows the railroad track that is shown on the sectional leaving La Junta, Colorado (SFM3) to the southwest of the edge of the Wichita-S sectional. Look for the track as it reappears on the Denver-S sectional at the very northeast corner.

Waypoint ID:	SF03
Waypoint Name:	Council Grove
Sectional:	Kansas City-N
Latitude:	38° 39′ N
Longitude:	96° 30′ W
Next Waypoint:	SF04
Bearing to Next:	255°
Range to Next:	11.9 nm
Days on the Trail:	8

Cautions: Herington (HRU).

From Council Grove, it was a day's travel to Diamond Spring. Make a mental note of the distance and the time that it takes you to fly this section. This will give you a sense of the rate of progress that the wagons experienced (an average of 2 miles an hour).

Route from SF03 to SF04

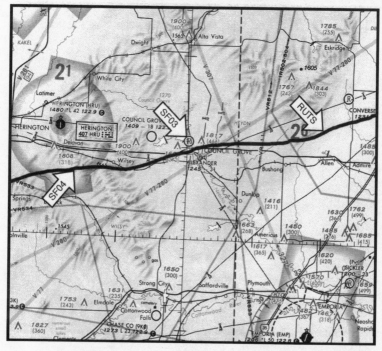

Council Grove

In 1825 at Council Grove, the government surveyor, George Sibley, signed a treaty with the Osage Indians in which the Indians agreed—for $800-worth of trade goods—to allow the whitemen to cross their territory in peace. The signing took place under a huge oak tree that survived until the 1950s. The actual sight is just east of town where the Little John Creek crosses Rt. 56. Near here the wagons would group into larger caravans that afforded greater protection from Indian attacks.

Nearby is the grave of Father Juan de Padilla, a member of Coronado's expedition of the 1540s, who stayed behind to serve the Indians' spiritual needs but was soon killed.

Waypoint ID:	SF06
Waypoint Name:	Durham Ruts
Sectional:	Wichita-N
Latitude:	38° 28´ N
Longitude:	97° 15´ W
Next Waypoint:	SF07
Bearing to Next:	247°
Range to Next:	33.8 nm
Days on the Trail:	14

Cautions: McPherson (MPR).

Several sections of ruts are visible near the Little Arkansas River crossing. Take the time to locate the ruts and notice the split in the Trail just east of the Arkansas River (SF07).

Route from SF06 to SF07

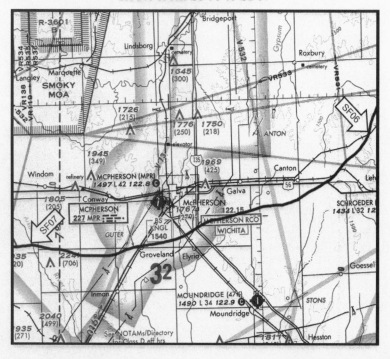

Durham Ruts

The Durham ruts are a fine example of ruts that have been preserved over time. They run parallel to the railroad tracks on the north side. The scars are visible from several miles away and you can compare the different appearances the scars can have after many years. There are eroded scars, depressions, and vegetation demarcations all intermixed along the several miles of ruts.

This is a good place to experiment. Fly over the ruts at different altitudes to see the difference that just a few hundred feet can make in the way the ruts appear (and disappear) with changing light conditions and altitude. This exercise will pay off when you approach Willow Bar (SF12) where it takes a sharp eye to spot the scars as they ascend the ridge to the south.

Waypoint ID:	SF05
Waypoint Name:	Lost Spring
Sectional:	Wichita-N
Latitude:	38° 34´ N
Longitude:	97° 00´ W
Next Waypoint:	SF06
Bearing to Next:	238°
Range to Next:	13.2 nm
Days on the Trail:	12

Cautions: Rising terrain.

     Watch for a small section of ruts just to the south of the spring. From Lost Spring, the Trail passes through Tampa then turns toward Durham. There are some significant ruts near Cottonwood Crossing (shown on the map). The Durham Ruts parallel the R.R. on the north side of the tracks.

Route from SF05 to SF06

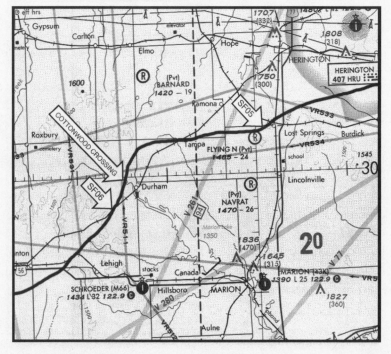

Lost Spring

Lost Spring is still visible today. Conveniently located one day away from Diamond Spring, the area around the spring provided good grass for the first wagons of the season. Along the Trail, much of the water was obtained from streams that were often muddy. Farther to the west, the water became alkaline and more contaminated with biological impurities. The people of the 1800s had little or no knowledge of bacteria. This was true in the cities as well as on the Trail. Thousands died in the cities from drinking water that contained the Asiatic Cholera pathogen as well as many other waterborne diseases.

Waypoint ID:	SF04
Waypoint Name:	Diamond Spring
Sectional:	Kansas City-N
Latitude:	38° 37´ N
Longitude:	96° 45´ W
Next Waypoint:	SF05
Bearing to Next:	250°
Range to Next:	12.1 nm
Days on the Trail:	11

Cautions: Herington (HRU).

Route from SF04 to SF05

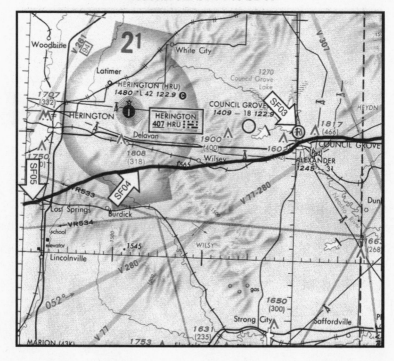

RUTS

Diamond Spring Ranch

Sibley, the surveyor, named this spring after he perceived it as a "Diamond in the Plains." The spring was of major importance to the caravans and many of the journals specifically mention it by name. Several of the streams to the west were named for their relative distance from this spring. Today the spring is on private property and has been capped for a domestic water source.

Fresh, clean water was a precious resource along the Trail. Huge quantities were needed to water the livestock; this is one of the reasons that the Trail follows streams and rivers for much of the way. The riverbeds also were relatively flat and ran in the right direction.

Watch for a set of ruts ascending the hill to the west of the spring. Notice the difference between the modern dirt road and the grassy swales just to the north of the road that is marked on the photo.

Waypoint ID:	SF07
Waypoint Name:	Little Arkansas River
Sectional:	Wichita-N
Latitude:	38° 18´ N
Longitude:	97° 56´ W
Next Waypoint:	SF08
Bearing to Next:	274°
Range to Next:	22.4 nm
Days on the Trail:	18

Cautions: Lyons-Rice (LYO). Watch for parachute activity near Lyons.

Cross to the north side of Rt. 56 two miles west of Chase and watch for Ralph's Ruts to the west.

Route from SF07 to SF08

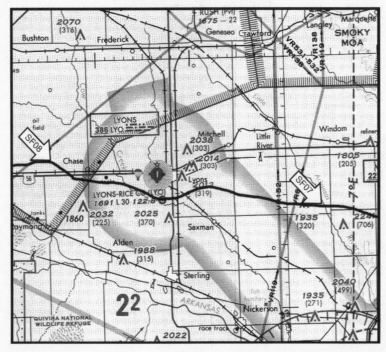

Arkansas River Crossing

River crossings were unpredictable. The flow of water in the rivers was not controlled by dams, and a storm to the west could turn a slow, meandering flow into a torrent that would last for days. Wagons often had to be double or triple teamed to pull them through the mud and sand bottoms. These crossings always slowed the progress of the wagons. If the water was high, the current could be deadly to the men who were trying to drive the wagons across. Steep banks had to be excavated into ramps to allow the wagons to roll down and back up the other side. Ramps made by a previous caravan would have been washed away in the first flood.

Waypoint ID:	SF08
Waypoint Name:	Ralph's Ruts
Sectional:	Wichita-N
Latitude:	38° 22´ N
Longitude:	98° 24´ W
Next Waypoint:	SF09
Bearing to Next:	248°
Range to Next:	40.1 nm
Days on the Trail:	21

Cautions: Great Bend (GBD) and Larned (LQR) are **very close** to the route.

If you plan to land at Larned, take the time to overfly Fort Larned and the Santa Fe Trail Center before you land.

Please avoid low level overflights that may disturb ground visitors.

Route from SF08 to SF09

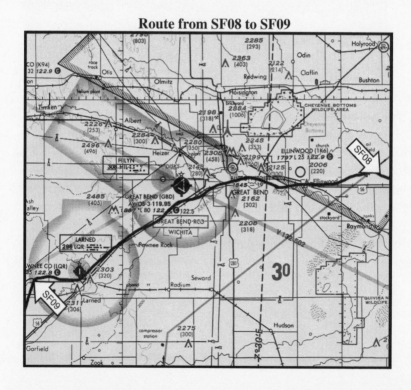

Ralph's Ruts

Plum Buttes, near Ralph's Ruts, were really sand hills that were surrounded by plum trees in Trail days. They could be seen from several miles to the east and served as a landmark for navigation. The lucky travelers who arrived when the fruit was ripening enjoyed a variation in their diet that undoubtedly caused some stomach distress for those who overindulged. The plum trees remain today, but the buttes were eroded away in the early 1900s.

Ralph's Ruts are aligned east to west and pass through a small pond before continuing west for a half mile through a long narrow pasture. Look for the pond and the ruts will become evident.

Waypoint ID:	SF09
Waypoint Name:	Fort Larned
Sectional:	Wichita-N
Latitude:	38° 11′ N
Longitude:	99° 13′ W
Next Waypoint:	SF10
Bearing to Next:	240°
Range to Next:	58.5 nm
Days on the Trail:	25

Cautions: Kinsley (33K), Dodge City (DDC) and Cimarron (8K8) are very near the route.

At the bend in the river, to the south near Ford, there are some ruts on the north bank (see map).

Route from SF09 to SF10

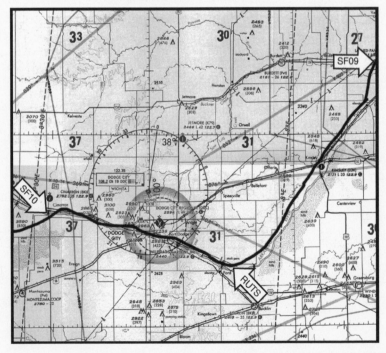

Fort Larned

Larned is home to the Santa Fe Trail Center and Fort Larned (both are along Rt. 56 west of town). Either attraction is worthy of a stop, but having both in the same town makes this stop a must! If you take time to overfly the fort before you land, locating it on the ground will be even easier. The National Park Service is becoming more sensitive about noisy airplanes disturbing the ambience of their parks, monuments and historic sites, and they have requested that readers be asked to maintain the 2000 foot minimums above these features. Fort Larned, Bent's Old Fort and Fort Union are all managed by the National Park Service. Because these sites occupy relatively small areas, the views from the air are wonderful from a mile away and 2000 feet AGL. Your cooperation on this matter will be appreciated by the Park Service and ground visitors.

Waypoint ID:	SF10	
Waypoint Name:	Cimarron, KS	
Sectional:	Wichita-S	
Latitude:	37° 48´ N	
Longitude:	100° 21´ W	
Next Waypoint:	SF11 *or*	SFM1
Bearing to Next:	236°	285°
Range to Next:	54.1 nm	26.5 nm
Days on the Trail:	30	

Cautions: Ulysses (ULS).

At Cimarron the Trail splits into the shorter Cimarron Route (across the desert to the southwest, known as the *Jornada*) and the longer Mountain Route through Bent's Old Fort along the river. **If you choose to follow the Mountain Route, go to waypoint SFM1 next.**

Route from SF10 to SF11

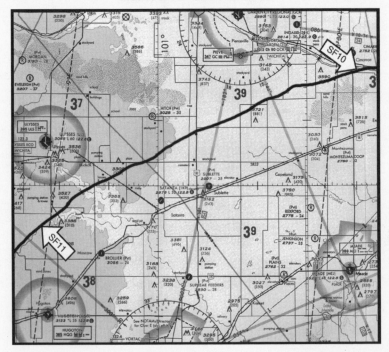

Cimarron, Kansas

There were several cutoffs and river crossings in the area. The easternmost was at Ford and the westernmost was upstream near Syracuse. All would eventually rejoin the Cimarron Route at various locations along the Cimarron River.

Due to farming efforts, few ruts survive between the Arkansas River and the Cimarron River. The lush farmland below you was a waterless desert before deep wells provided the irrigation water that has transformed the landscape. Since the land is relatively flat, the route is nearly a straight line to Wagon Bed Spring (SF11).

(To avoid confusion, please note that both Cimarron, Kansas (SF10), and Cimarron, New Mexico (SFM5), are waypoints.)

Waypoint ID:	SF11
Waypoint Name:	Wagon Bed Spring
Sectional:	Wichita-S
Latitude:	37° 24´ N
Longitude:	101° 22´ W
Next Waypoint:	SF12
Bearing to Next:	231°
Range to Next:	52.3 nm
Days on the Trail:	35

Cautions: Elkhart (EHA).

Watch for ruts just to the east of the spring and to the southwest near the "oil" wells that are marked on the sectional.

Route from SF11 to SF12

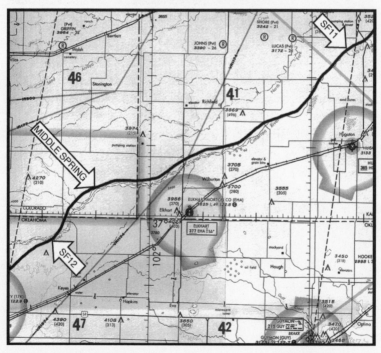

Wagon Bed Spring

Wagon Bed Spring was known as the Lower Spring until an unknown traveler buried an old wagon bed in the spring to provide a reservoir for the water. This spring was the first water since leaving the Arkansas 60 miles to the northeast. The next dependable source of water was 36 miles upstream at Middle Spring (see map).

This series of springs provided the only dependable water, since the river was dry most of the year. Where there were no springs, some travelers were able to dig shallow wells along the river bed and were rewarded with polluted and alkaline water. But with no other source of water, those shallow wells often meant the difference between life and death.

Waypoint ID:	SF12
Waypoint Name:	Willow Bar
Sectional:	Wichita-S
Latitude:	36° 57´ N
Longitude:	102° 18´ W
Next Waypoint:	SF13
Bearing to Next:	238°
Range to Next:	40.2 nm
Days on the Trail:	39

Cautions: Boise City (17K).

At Willow Bar take time to locate the ruts that ascend the ridge to the south and lead you to Las Vegas, NM. They can be hard to see if the light is not just right.

Route from SF12 to SF13

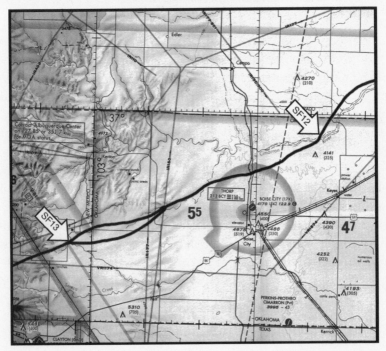

The Santa Fe Trail by Air

Willow Bar

At Willow Bar the real thrill of the trip begins. The ruts that ascend the ridge to the south are almost continuous for the next 100 miles. The appearance of the wagon scars changes as the ruts cross different soil and vegetation types. This area is the perfect place to perfect your skills at recognizing ruts. Take the time to drift to the sides of the Trail and look for sections of ruts left by the wagons that had to leave the main track to find grass and fuel. Many of these are not mapped—finding them can provide the excitement of discovery.

The main route divides into a maze of ruts several miles east of SF13, the next waypoint. It is fun to try to spot as many of these well-defined variations as you can. If you are traveling with young ones, the thrill of the search should help spark any waning interest.

Waypoint ID:	SF13
Waypoint Name:	McNees Crossing
Sectional:	Wichita-S
Latitude:	36° 41´ N
Longitude:	103° 04´ W
Next Waypoint:	SF14
Bearing to Next:	242°
Range to Next:	27.3 nm
Days on the Trail:	43

Cautions: Clayton (CAO) and Mt. Dora MOAs. Call FSS for status.

     Watch for the automobile pull-off on the west side of Rt. 64/ 87 between Grenville and Mt. Dora. There is a monument here that notes the crossing of the Trail, for those bound by gravity to the highways.

Route from SF13 to SF14

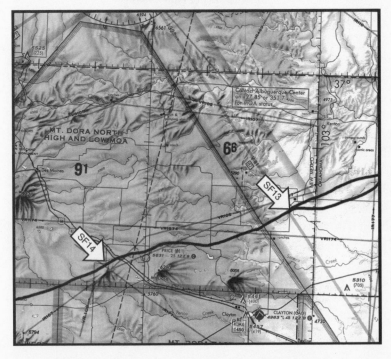

Ruts near McNees Crossing

McNees Crossing is where two young traders were killed by Indians in 1828 as they rested along the dry river bed. (The incident is mentioned in the "diary.") The reason this place was used as a crossing is obvious from the air. Notice the multiple ruts in the area.

This area is much the same as it was in the 1800s. The effects of agricultural "improvement" are minimal. Notice the desolation and the lack of fuel wood. In the distance, the landmarks called "Rabbitears Mountain" and "Point of Rocks" were coming into view of the caravans. Round Mountain will be the most visible from the air and the ruts pass just to the north of the volcanic cone.

Waypoint ID:	SF14
Waypoint Name:	Round Mountain
Sectional:	Wichita-S
Latitude:	36° 32′ N
Longitude:	103° 36′ W
Next Waypoint:	SF15
Bearing to Next:	248°
Range to Next:	26.5 nm
Days on the Trail:	45

Cautions: Mt. Dora MOAs.

Watch for abandoned foundations along the route as you approach Point of Rocks. These were stage stations during the later days of the Trail's history.

Route from SF14 to SF15

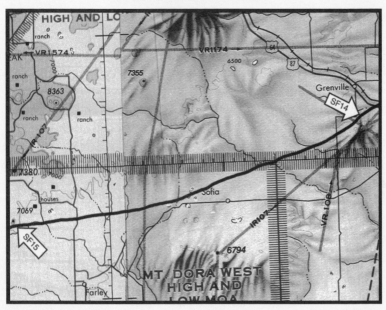

Round Mountain

Rising above the plains, Round Mountain (known as Mount Clayton today) and Mt. Dora are actually volcanic cones. The views from the top offered the Indians ample notice of approaching wagon trains.

This entire area provides a unique study in geology. From a greater altitude than you are probably flying, the distinct radial pattern of the drainage streams that originate near the tops of these cones clearly indicates their location.

The gravelly plains preserve the ruts well because the limited amount of moisture that falls here is rapidly absorbed, except in torrential downpours. The flatness of the area inhibits rapid runoff which washes away the ruts in other areas. Depressions caused by the wagon wheels collect what little water there is and the vegetation is totally different from the vegetation that grows in the surrounding area.

Waypoint ID:	SF15
Waypoint Name:	Point of Rocks
Sectional:	Denver-S
Latitude:	36° 26´ N
Longitude:	104° 08´ W
Next Waypoint:	SF16
Bearing to Next:	236°
Range to Next:	19.5 nm
Days on the Trail:	48

Cautions: Mt. Dora MOAs. Watch your altitude. The terrain is rising at an increasing rate.

Between the "Point" and the Canadian River, the ruts disappear as the Trail descends into the river flats. The steeper grade of the ground magnifies the effects of erosion which has washed away the scars.

Route from SF15 to SF16

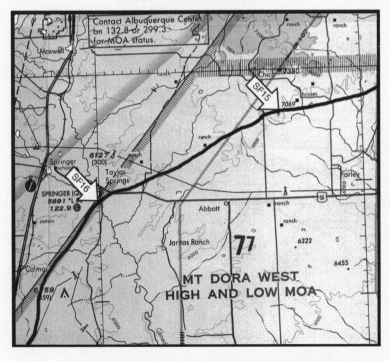

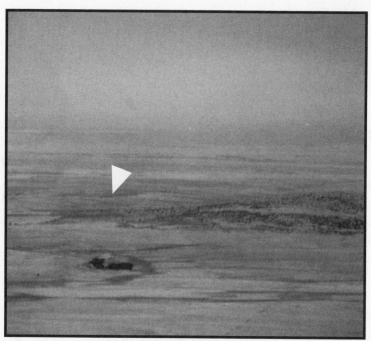

Point of Rocks, New Nexico

This is one of several landmarks along the Trail that was named "Point of Rocks." As with any rock outcropping along the route, it was covered with names and dates by early graffiti artists who felt compelled to mark their passing at any available opportunity. Some of the names here are of travelers massacred by Indians who liked to wait in ambush in the rocks. The largest cemetery (11 graves) on the Trail is at this landmark.

Notice that the Trail split several miles to the east of the "Point." As you pass the outcropping, the Trail rejoins and heads to the west. The ruts disappear as the Trail drops over the bluff to the Canadian River valley. Maintain your heading—the ruts will reappear in a few miles.

Waypoint ID:	SF16
Waypoint Name:	Canadian River
Sectional:	Denver-S
Latitude:	36° 18´ N
Longitude:	104-°30´ W
Next Waypoint:	SF17
Bearing to Next:	202°
Range to Next:	20.0 nm
Days on the Trail:	50

Cautions: Springer (Q42).

      Watch for a microwave tower on the bluff to the west.

Watch your altitude! If you are flying this section more than 3 hours after sunrise, get ready for some turbulence ahead.

Route from SF16 to SF17

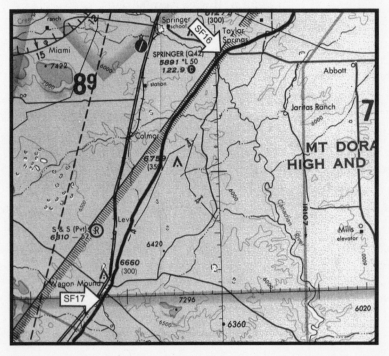

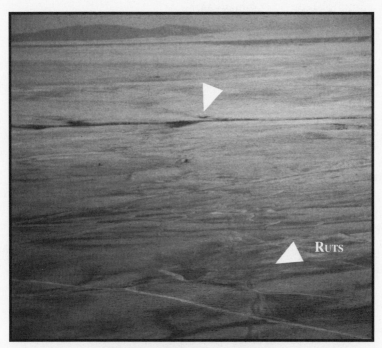

The Canadian River Crossing
(Wagon Mound in the Distance)

The Canadian River valley was a welcome source of water and fresh grass. This rock-bottomed river crossing was used because the river drops into the gorge downstream and the sandy bottom upstream would have been difficult to cross.

In the early years of the Trail, riders would ride ahead from here to Las Vegas and negotiate import taxes with Mexican officials. The area residents would bring wagons of fresh melons, squash, onions and peppers—a welcomed variation to the by-now bland diet of dried meat and breads. The men rested, and so did the livestock that had survived the crossing on sparse dried grasses and limited water.

Waypoint ID:	SF17
Waypoint Name:	Wagon Mound
Sectional:	Denver-S
Latitude:	36° 01´ N
Longitude:	104° 43´ W
Next Waypoint:	SF18
Bearing to Next:	215°
Range to Next:	18.4 nm
Days on the Trail:	52

Cautions: Turbulence area. Watch for thunderstorms that can materialize almost instantly over the mountains to the west. Wagon Mound is the larger outcropping east of town. The smaller outcroppings to the west of town are called "Pilot Knobs."

Between here and Las Vegas, watch for the best example of multiple ruts that remains along the Trail.

Route from SF17 to SF18

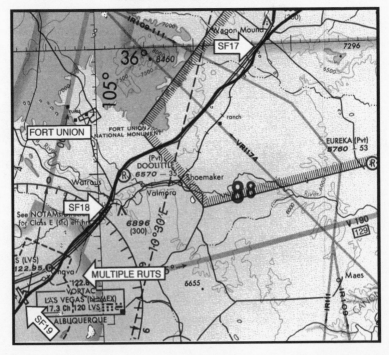

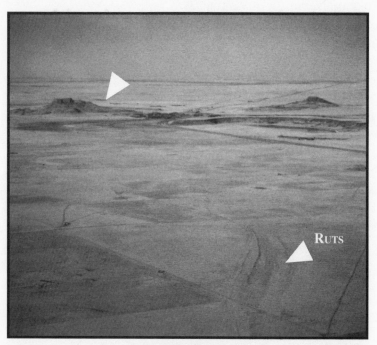

RUTS

Wagon Mound

Wagon Mound was a long-awaited landmark that meant Santa Fe and the end of the trip was only a week away. The "Mound" is what remains of a volcanic flow that filled an ancient valley. The ridges that formed the sides of the valley have eroded away, leaving the more resistant igneous rock. This area was another favorite ambush site for the Indians who would wait near the spring on the western slope for unsuspecting wagons.

As you approach from the east, look hard and you may be able to see the resemblance to a team of oxen pulling a wagon—a vision seen by the early traders who named the landmark. The higher in the air you are, the harder it is to see the resemblance.

Waypoint ID:	SF18
Waypoint Name:	Watrous, NM
Sectional:	Denver-S
Latitude:	35° 48′ N
Longitude:	104° 59′ W
Next Waypoint:	SF19
Bearing to Next:	209°
Range to Next:	11.6 nm
Days on the Trail:	54 via Cimarron Route
	61 via Mountain Route

Cautions: Turbulence and mountain wave rotors.

Notice the ruts in all directions. Take the time to fly over Fort Union (see map).

Route from SF18 to SF19

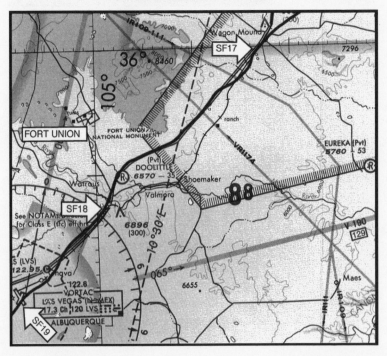

Watrous, New Mexico

Watrous was known as "La Junta" (the junction) in Trail days because the Mountain Route and the Cimarron Route rejoined there to continue to Santa Fe. The ruts that seem to come from all directions are a combination of Trail ruts and those of later stage-coach and military routes.

Watrous (as it became known after the arrival of the railroad) served as a staging area, much like Council Grove to the east, where eastbound wagons would wait until there were enough wagons to form a caravan big enough to provide safety from Indian attacks. The small community thrived as a supply center for the soldiers after Fort Union was established.

Waypoint ID:	SF19
Waypoint Name:	Las Vegas Airport
Sectional:	Denver-S
Latitude:	35° 39´ N
Longitude:	105° 08´ W
Next Waypoint:	SF20
Bearing to Next:	263°
Range to Next:	40.0 nm
Days on the Trail:	55 via Cimarron Route
	62 via Mountain Route

Cautions: It is easy to inadvertently fly into the Las Vegas (LVS) airport traffic area while looking at the ruts.

LVS is the best place to land if you are planning to visit Fort Union. (*If* you have reserved a car!)

Route from SF19 to SF20

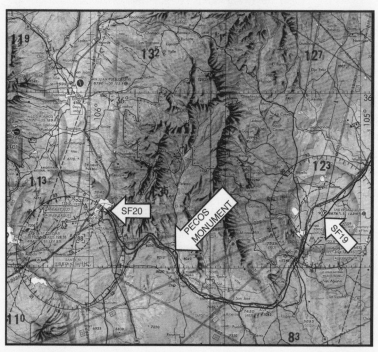

RUTS

Airport, Las Vegas, New Mexico

At the south end of the runway at LVS is an excellent example of multiple ruts. The wagons often traveled several columns wide so they could form a defensive perimeter in the event of attack and so no single wagon would be in the vulnerable position of last in line. A quick attack from the rear could be over and the Indians already be gone before the front wagons could turn around and join the defense.

If you have the time, land and take the afternoon to drive to Fort Union and to visit some of the historical buildings in downtown Las Vegas. The town has 900 buildings on federal or state historical registries and it was here that Kearney declared (in 1846) that the New Mexico Territory belonged to the United States.

Waypoint ID:	SF20
Waypoint Name:	Santa Fe, NM (City)
Sectional:	Denver-S and
	Albuquerque-N
Latitude:	35° 41´ N
Longitude:	105° 57´ W
Next Waypoint:	none
Days on the Trail:	58 via Cimarron Route
	65 via Mountain Route

Cautions: If you are from the "East," the term "density altitude" will take on a new meaning here. Check POH for leaning procedures to be used before landing! Density altitudes can exceed 11,000 ft at Santa Fe and more than a few planes have gotten wrinkled trying to land at "full rich."

Notice Location of Airport Relative to the City

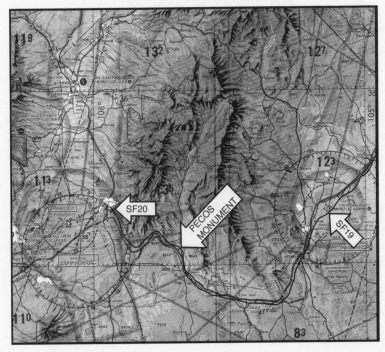

Airport, Santa Fe, New Mexico

      The Santa Fe airport can be difficult to locate in some light conditions. The safest bet is to go to the VOR and then track in to the airport. Little sign of the Trail is visible from the air so your attention can be directed to traffic avoidance.

      One of the highlights of a stop in Santa Fe is the opportunity to fly a MIG, a YAK and an L-29 Delfin jet at Fantasy Fighters. They also offer aerobatics training and mountain flying instruction. A more detailed description of their courses is included in the Appendix. If the pilots want to indulge in their fantasies, Santa Fe offers a wonderful diversion for non-pilot members of your party.

Mountain Route

Waypoint ID:	SFM1
Waypoint Name:	Garden City, KS
Sectional:	Wichita-N
Latitude:	37° 58´ N
Longitude:	100° 52´ W
Next Waypoint:	SFM2
Bearing to Next:	267°
Range to Next:	89.6 nm
Days on the Trail:	33

Cautions: Lakin (36K), Syracuse (3K3) and Lamar (LAA) are all very near the route.

Watch for a herd of buffalo to the south of town.

Route from SF10 to SFM1 to SFM2

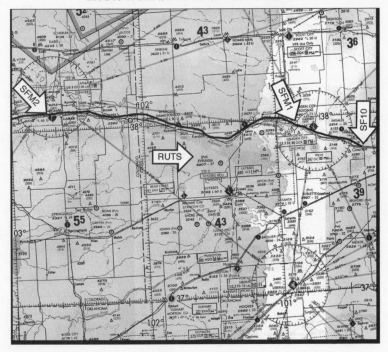

Garden City, Kansas

The Mountain Route has fewer signs of the Trail that are visible from the air, so there are fewer waypoints used along its course. It does pass Bent's Old Fort, one of the highlights of the trip.

This Trail branch was developed in the early 1840s because water was more readily available and the Indians were less of a threat. In the 1860s this route was used to avoid the Confederate armies that roamed the southern territory. Prior to use as the Santa Fe Trail, the route had been used for years by mountain men who traded with the Indians of the Rockies.

The route of the Trail followed the path of least resistance up the river valley, as does the railroad that parallels the route.

Waypoint ID:	SFM2
Waypoint Name:	Bent's New Fort
Sectional:	Wichita-N
Latitude:	38° 05´ N
Longitude:	102° 45´ W
Next Waypoint:	SFM3
Bearing to Next:	256°
Range to Next:	32.5 nm
Days on the Trail:	40

Caution: Las Animas—City/County (7V9) and La Junta (LHX) are just off the route.

The remains of Bent's New Fort are just foundation outlines and a pile of rubble, so do not waste too much time looking for them.

Route from SFM2 to SFM3

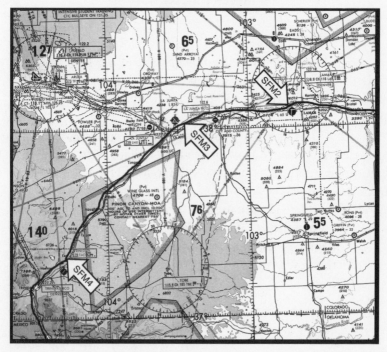

Bent's New Fort

Although called a "fort," Bent's Fort was not a military installation. William Bent, his brother Charles, and a Frenchman named Ceran St. Vrain saw an opportunity to profit from the growing fur trade in the mountain west. In 1833 they built a trading post 30 miles west of here to buy furs from the trappers and to resupply these early explorers. Business was brisk until 1849 when William burned the fort and relocated 30 miles downstream (Bent's New Fort) in an attempt to expand his market to the busy Cimarron cutoff.

The National Park Service has restored the original "fort" and named it "Bent's Old Fort" (SFM3).

Waypoint ID:	SFM3
Waypoint Name:	Bent's Old Fort
Sectional:	Wichita-N
Latitude:	38° 02´ N
Longitude:	103° 26´ W
Next Waypoint:	SFM4
Bearing to Next:	213°
Range to Next:	57.9 nm
Days on the Trail:	44

Cautions: Trinidad (TAD)

La Junta (LHX) is where you land to see Bent's Old Fort. Watch gusting winds!

Take the time to fly over the fort before you land.

Please avoid low level overflights that may disturb ground visitors.

Route from SFM3 to SFM4

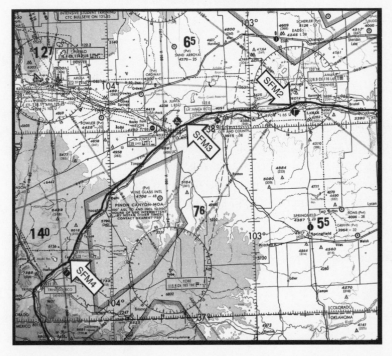

The restored fort is run by the National Park Service as a National Historic Site and is a wonderful example of what well-spent tax dollars can provide. Interpretive guides dress in period clothing and actually operate the restored blacksmith shop and carpentry shop during the busy season. Plan to spend at least half a day here because government spending cuts may soon cause this monument to the past to go the way of the Santa Fe Trail—existing only in our memories.

Wear comfortable walking shoes, and if you go in the spring or summer, take along bug dope. If you plan to spend the night, get your motel room early because the time will pass quickly at the fort and the motels fill early during the peak season.

Waypoint ID:	SFM4
Waypoint Name:	Trinidad Ruts
Sectional:	Denver-S
Latitude:	37° 19´ N
Longitude:	104° 15´ W
Next Waypoint:	SFM5
Bearing to Next:	204°
Range to Next:	57.7 nm
Days on the Trail:	50

Cautions: Trinidad (TAD) is just south of the ruts.

Turbulence will become more of a problem as you approach the mountains. Cross over Raton Pass with caution and plenty of altitude. There is little sign of the Trail until you get close to the Raton airport so enjoy the sights from plenty of altitude.

Route from SFM4 to SFM5

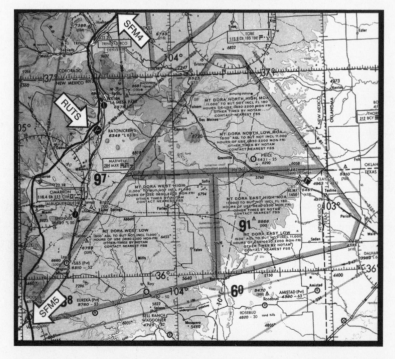

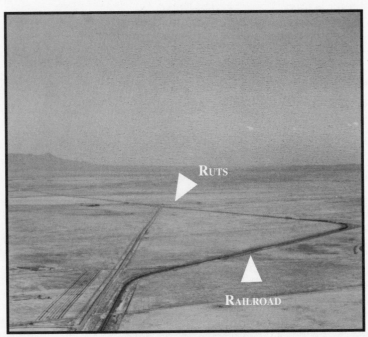

The Trinidad Ruts

You have been following the railroad tracks for some time now. This railroad was responsible for the demise of the old Trail as a major freight route. From the Trail's beginning as a marketing channel in 1821 when Becknell, using three wagons, took $3000 worth of goods to Santa Fe and returned with a 2000% profit, until 1873 when the railroad reached Trinidad, the Trail was responsible for millions of dollars worth of goods reaching not only Santa Fe but well into Mexico's market area. The arrival here of the railhead essentially eliminated the functional life of the Cimarron cutoff. The Trail was a pathway to an existing under-supplied market area, not a means of exploration. Unlike the Oregon Trail which primarily moved people, the Santa Fe Trail moved freight. But, the railroad moved freight faster and cheaper.

Waypoint ID:	SFM5
Waypoint Name:	Cimarron, NM
Sectional:	Denver-S
Latitude:	36° 31´ N
Longitude:	104° 55´ W
Next Waypoint:	SF18
Bearing to Next:	174°
Range to Next:	43.1 nm
Days on the Trail:	57

Cautions: La Mesa (Q65) and Raton (RTN) are along the route.
Excellent ruts are preserved at the western edge of the
Raton airport. Watch the winds and turbulence.

From Cimarron, the route rejoins the Cimarron Route at
Watrous. Follow the ruts to Fort Union and then to Watrous (SF18).

Route from SFM5 to SF18

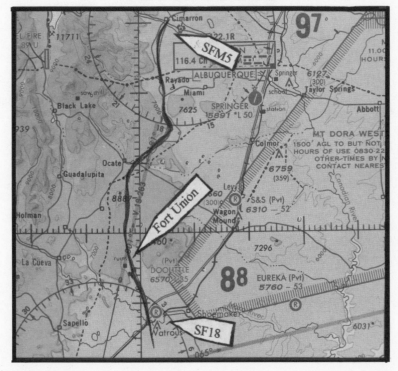

Cimarron, New Mexico

Cimarron was founded along the Mountain Route in 1841 and soon began to take its place in the history of the West. Guest registers from the early hotels read like a "Who's Who." Outlaws passed in and out of town on a daily basis. Buffalo Bill Cody organized his *Wild West Show* here. The downtown area has been named a National Historic District and is worth the time to visit.

Between this historic town and Raton is the National Rifle Association's Whittington Center which hosts 70,000 visitors a year. Several miles to the south is the Philmont Scout Ranch and a herd of buffalo that can often be seen between the ranch buildings (marked on the Denver sectional as two black dots along the 225° radial of the CIM VOR) and the road to Rayado.

APPENDIX

Appendix
Contents

Appendix Introduction

The information listed on the following pages was correct at the time of publication. Because of fluctuating prices and other conditions beyond our control, use the information as a guideline only.

Evaluations of FBOs and other services were made based upon the treatment received before the providers knew this guide was being written. Those that have offered to provide special considerations for our readers reserve the right to change or withdraw those considerations without notice.

Those FBOs that offer courtesy cars do so as a *courtesy!* Please call ahead to check the availability of those cars and any special regulations that might affect their usage.

Many of the towns and cities along the route have a very active chamber of commerce. A call or letter will result in a packet of information that contains more details and current information than a guide like this could possibly provide. The chambers' phone numbers are listed under the appropriate town heading.

Car rental rates are sometimes much cheaper if you call the 800 numbers and ask for the "best available rate" than if you just walk in off the street. The 800 numbers are included for those agencies that have outlets at the major stops along the Trail. Local numbers are listed under the appropriate town to aid cancellations and verifications as well as unexpected arrivals. (In our experience, the 800 numbers often say no cars are available, but the local numbers will have cars.) Independent car rental agencies are also listed when available. Shop prices carefully. We have found rate differences of as much as *400%.*

Detailed Waypoint Information to
The Santa Fe Trail Center and Fort Larned

Larned, Kansas
The Santa Fe Trail Center and Fort Larned
Access Airports:
> Larned; Pawnee County(LQR)
> Great Bend (GBD)

As with most of the stops along the Trail, ground transportation is the greatest problem. Because Avis has an outlet at the Great Bend airport, I have always landed there. The 20-mile drive from Great Bend to Larned is worth the convenience of dependable car availability.

Larned is home to both the Santa Fe Trail Center and Fort Larned and is well worth the time to visit. Both facilities are on the main road out of Larned to the west and easy to find. Follow the signs to Fort Larned and you will pass right in front of the Center.

The Santa Fe Trail Center has a small, privately funded museum with some fine exhibits relating to Trail days. If you are traveling with young ones, there is plenty of room for them to run off steam. The Center is also the headquarters of the Santa Fe Trail Association and provides an excellent library for serious researchers of Trail history. Reproductions of a sod house and a dugout house provide an insight into life on the prairie. Actual wagons that were used on the Trail are on display with a variety of other related treasures.

Fort Larned is one of the stops that you should not miss. The fort has a unique history. After being abandoned by the military and sold to private interests, the fort served as a ranch headquarters for 80 years. In the 1960s, the National Park Service purchased the property and began the restoration. The detail of the restoration is amazing. The living quarters of the troops looks just like it must have in the 1860s. The greatest treat appears as you walk into the barracks. An elderly gentleman appears from the shadows, dressed in military attire of the period. As he begins to talk, you are transported back in time. A most riveting account of life at the fort unfolds with details that you will retell at parties for years to come.

The best part of his presentation is the enthusiasm with which this charming gentleman presents the facts. The hour that I spent with George Varner as he shared the details of military life was one of the best hours of the trip. George retired from the U.S. Postal Service on a Friday several years ago. The next morning he and his wife Zelda departed for the fort to volunteer their time to enhance the quality of the visitor's experience. If you are lucky enough to visit the fort when George is on duty, it will be an experience that you will not forget. After you visit the fort, I hope you will join me in a heartfelt "Thanks" to all the folks who volunteer their time at this and the other sites.

Fort Larned Hours:

    8 a.m. to 5 p.m. daily except Thanksgiving, Christmas and New Year's Day.

Fees: $2.00 Adults

Address:

    Fort Larned National Historic Site

    Route 3

    Larned, Kansas 67550

Phone: 316-285-6911

Fax: 316-285-3571

Directions to the site:

    The fort is located 6 miles west of Larned on Rt. 56. The drive seems a lot farther than 6 miles so be patient. The site is well marked with signs. Keep an eye out for the Santa Fe Trail Center on the left as you go toward the fort.

La Junta, Colorado
Bent's Old Fort
Access Airport:
La Junta (LHX)

Bent's Old Fort is a reconstruction of the private counterpart of Fort Larned. The "fort" was built in 1833 by Charles and William Bent and their partner Ceran St. Vrain to capitalize on the fur trade of the Rocky Mountain area. As the Santa Fe Trail became more popular, the emphasis on supplying merchant caravans increased with the declining fur trade in the late 1830s. The Bents were significant influences in establishing peaceful relations with the Indians of the southern plains. The fort served as the major trading center and source of supply for Indians and mountain men. For many years the fort was the first place along the Santa Fe Trail Mountain Route to have wagons repaired or to resupply the necessities of everyday living for the teamsters.

Unlike the un-walled Fort Larned, Bent's Old Fort is more like the "forts" that we have come to expect from television renditions of the West. From atop the adobe walls the views of the surrounding area are much the same as the Bents enjoyed in the 1800s. Small cannons are mounted at strategic places around the perimeter of the fort. During the reconstruction, great attention was paid to detail. Historical interpreters in period garb add a feeling of authenticity to the blacksmith shop and the carpenter shop. During the busy season, craftsmen re-enact the work done in the shops.

As you wander through the many rooms, a feeling of what life was like in 1845 begins to displace the hustle and bustle of modern times. About the time that you form the conclusion that "life must have been incredibly hard," you will discover a room with a beautiful billiard table. After the first shock wears off, the question "How did they get this here?" pops to mind. The trade room has an excellent display of the favored trade goods of the time. The book store and gift shop offer replicas of some of the goods that the Indians and trappers traveled many miles to obtain—in exchange for a fur or two.

If this is your first trip to the Southwest, pay attention to the feel of the adobe building. The rooms have huge logs (called *vigas)* for ceiling beams. This detail, along with the feeling of foot-thick walls is a good introduction to the architecture of the New Mexico area. In contrast to the primitive living conditions depicted, small tokens of civilization sparkle from the hidden corners of the darkened rooms. For many years during the Trail days, the fort was the first "civilization" the travelers had seen in over a month. The amenities were welcome luxuries that were enjoyed for several days while the livestock grazed and regained their strength.

Bent's Old Fort Hours:

> 8 a.m. to 5:30 p.m. daily from Memorial Day to Labor Day;
> 9 a.m. to 4 p.m. daily from Labor Day to Memorial Day,
> except Thanksgiving, Christmas and New Year's Day.
> Tours and demonstrations are conducted at various times.

Fees: $2.00—Adults; Under 17—Free

Address:

> Bent's Old Fort National Historic Site
> 35110 Highway 194 E
> La Junta, Colorado 81050

Phone: 719-384-2596

Fax: 719-384-2615

Directions to the fort:

> The fort is easy to find and only 8 miles from town. Ask Jake or the attendant on duty at the airport for directions. Wear comfortable walking shoes and take bug dope, sunscreen, a camera and a picnic lunch. The fort is an easy place to spend the better part of a day.

Las Vegas, New Mexico
Fort Union
Access Airport:
Las Vegas (LVS)

Fort Union is unlike the two previous forts. The remains of the structures are being preserved and not restored. The experience of walking among the remnants of old adobe walls with the warm, dry air blowing the flag straight out is different from that of walking the walls at Bent's Fort or listening to George at Fort Larned. The views in all directions offer a sense of the desolation and isolation that the early teamsters must have felt 150 years ago. The experience is a trip back in time, although in a different dimension than the other two stops.

The term "Fort Union" should actually be plural since there were three separate "forts." The first was built in 1851 and consisted of crude log shelters to house the troops that had been moved from Santa Fe. The fort provided better protection for the western end of the Trail, and got the troops out of the city, where they were prone to partake of unmilitary pleasures.

The second "fort" was built in 1861 to provide protection from the Confederate Forces that were expected to move into the area from Texas. The living quarters were still primitive but the earthworks were impressive. The remnants of the star-shaped fortification can be seen from the air at the southeast corner of the complex. After a brief skirmish at Pigeon Ranch (located between the fort and Santa Fe), the Confederates were driven from the area for the duration of the War. The fort was abandoned after the Civil War.

In 1863, construction of the final version was begun. Resuming the role of protector of the Trail, the fort became a supply depot for all the other forts in the southwest. Huge quantities of supplies came across the Trail and later the railroad, and as today, supplying the military became big business. The fort thrived until 1891 when it was abandoned.

An hour spent walking the pathways through the ghostly ruins is an hour well spent. The visitors center has a book store that is well stocked with literature about the Trail and life at that time. A leisurely drive back to Las Vegas through Mora, Ocate and Wagon

Mound (all to the north) will provide a view of the area that has not changed much since the wagons rolled across the bumpy Trail. A few more miles to the north you'll find Philmont Scout Ranch, a good stop if you have Boy Scouting in your blood. Farther yet to the north is the National Rifle Association Headquarters near Raton. The whole trip can easily be done in a day from either Santa Fe or Las Vegas.

The town of Las Vegas became a city because of economic activity spawned by military activity at the fort. The town boasts more than 900 buildings on state or federal historic registries. An hour or two spent in town will reveal some beautifully restored Victorian mansions. Contact the Chamber of Commerce for a packet that contains an excellent guide to these old homes.

Fort Union Hours:
> 8 a.m. to 5 p.m. daily except Christmas and New Year's Day.

Fees: $2.00—adults

Address:
> Fort Union National Monument
> Watrous, New Mexico 87753

Phone: 505-425-8025

Directions to the site:
The fort lies 26 miles northwest of Las Vegas. Use the sectional chart for a map and ask directions as there are several ways to reach the fort. There are no facilities at the fort except restrooms and picnic tables. Wear good walking shoes and take sunscreen and a camera.

Santa Fe, New Mexico
Santa Fe—End of the Trail
Access Airport:
Santa Fe (SAF)

Santa Fe is like no other place on Earth. Composed of a unique mixture of three cultures (Anglo, Spanish-Mexican and Indian), Santa Fe offers something for everyone.

Wander the "Plaza"; you'll move back in time when you visit the Palace of the Governors, the oldest continuously occupied building in the country. A few doors away may be a gallery of modern art or an apparel shop full of southwestern clothing. If your feet begin to tire, there is no better way to rest than to sit under a tree on the "Plaza" and watch the diverse collection of people that wander by. The many gift shops provide a staggering selection of treasures. Be sure to stop by Dressman's on the west side of the "Plaza." Frank and Linda offer some of the finest goodies in town. The south side of their store contains some wonderful Indian art that is truly collectible art.

As you continue your wanderings, you will notice a variety of eating establishments that is probably the most diverse you will find between New York and Los Angeles. If art is your forte, do not miss Canyon Road. In fact, do not miss this wonderful area even if art is not your forte. As the narrow street winds its way among the old adobe buildings, aromas drift from the doorways of some of the specialty shops that will betray their contents before you look in the windows. The smells of wonderful specialty foods will lure you to one of the open air cafes that line this world famous street. Among fresh flowers under clear blue skies, you will begin to understand why Santa Fe is called "The City Different."

The city has gone to great length to preserve the look and feel of "old" Santa Fe. Architectural styles and designs of the 17th and 18th century have been maintained in an attempt to capture forever the history of the city at the end of the Trail. Brick sidewalks, *portals, vigas* and walled courtyards create a feeling of warmth and coziness that set the city apart from others.

As wonderful as the city of Santa Fe is, it is only the beginning of the Santa Fe experience. The area within 60 miles of the Capital City contains eight Indian pueblos, Bandelier National

Monument and Los Alamos (home of the atomic bomb). In-depth description of these features is beyond the scope of this book, so please call or write the agencies listed later in the Appendix for complete information.

The moderate climate of the area contributes to a style of living that is very outdoor directed. A short drive to the ski area in the mountains to the east will provide vistas of the Rio Grande Valley that will rival those from your plane. A trip to the old mining town of Madrid will offer another glimpse into the past, as well as a sense of the ecology of the high mountain desert.

Santa Fe is located at the base of the Sangre de Cristo mountains at almost 7000 feet above sea level and is subject to rapid and drastic changes in the weather. Do not go far without a jacket, even in the heat of July. The UV rays are very intense at this elevation and skin can become sunburned in just minutes. Afternoon winds are the rule, so plan early departures and arrivals in your plane. Again, be aware of density altitudes that can approach 11,000 feet.

Tourism is a major industry and the area is very popular so be prepared for crowds at certain times of the year. NEVER depend on lodging or rental car availability without reservations. The travel guides listed later in the Appendix will offer information for reservations.

Airport Information

Great Bend Airport (GBD)

FBO Midwest Piper Sales
       Phone: 316-792-4349
       Fax: 316-792-6741
       Courtesy Car: Reserved for quick hops to town
       Car rental:
             AVIS: 1-800-331-1212
                   Local: 316-792-4042
             Marmie Dodge: 316-792-2571
       Motels with pickup:
             Best Western Angus Inn: 1-800-528-1234
                   Local: 316-792-3541
             Holiday Inn: 1-800-HOLIDAY
                   Local: 316-792-2431
             Super 8: 1-800-800-8000
                   Local: 316-793-8486
       Chamber of Commerce: 316-792-2401

Midwest Piper Sales still retains the concept of customer service. Windshields are _carefully_ cleaned without asking. Wing surfaces are protected during fueling operations and a large hangar generally has space if you are nervous about the notorious Kansas hail.

Inside, Ginnie's hospitality made me feel like she had me confused with someone she had known for years. A few minutes later I realized that she is one of those few people who really appreciate their customers. If you are looking for a souvenir to hang in your den, she has some beautiful wooden props for sale. Needless to say, if you need help with transportation or lodging, Ginnie will have the problem solved before you finish explaining it.

If you mention Western Airtrails, Ginnie will give you a discount on your fuel.

La Junta, Colorado
Bent's Old Fort **(LHX)**

FBO: LJM Aviation
      Phone: 719-384-8407
      Courtesy Car: **<u>A Must— Call ahead</u>**
      Car Rental: Ford Dealer—719-384-5421
        (Limited availability and expensive)
      Motel with pick up:
            Quality Inn: 1-800-228-5151
                    Local: 719-384-2571
      Motels:
            Super 8: 1-800-800-8000
                    Local: 719-384-4408
            Stagecoach Inn: 719-384-5476
            Midtown: 719-384-7741

      Chamber of Commerce: 719-384-7411

Local CFI: Floyd Austin 719-254-4509
      (Call ahead for an appointment for a 3-4 hour course on mountain flying. This seasoned mountain pilot is a check pilot for the CAP and has 20+ years of mountain flying experience.)

      The facilities at La Junta are what every pilot dreams about. The manager, Jake Freidenberger, is one of the most helpful people that I encountered on the trip. The city graciously provides a courtesy car but recommends that you call ahead for reservations. The FBO lounge provides the weather channel and a spacious lounge to wait out weather. The fuel prices were the most inexpensive that I encountered anywhere along the route. The FBO is open 24 hours so that your plane is never unattended. Hats off to the City of La Junta for a job well done.

Las Vegas, New Mexico (LVS)

FBO: Crowell Aviation
            Phone: 505-454-0881
            Courtesy Car: Available for quick hops to town **only.**
            Car Rental:
                    Highlands Ford: 505-425-7545
                    Highlands Wrecker: 505-425-8769
            Taxi: 505-454-1864
            Motels:
                    Super 8: 1-800-800-8000
                            Local: 505-425-5288
                    Regal: 505-454-1456
                    Scottish Inn: 505-425-9357
                    Plaza Hotel: 505-425-3591
            Chamber of Commerce: 1-800-832-5947

As usual, ground transportation will be the biggest problem. Both car rental firms are in the auto repair business and as could be expected, their customers' needs take precedence over car rentals to the public. Highlands Wrecker seems to be the most courteous and suggests that you call several days in advance and they will hold a car for you, pick you up at the airport and allow you to leave the car at the field when you depart.

Santa Fe, New Mexico (SAF)

The Santa Fe airport has two FBOs and they each approach the market differently. The usual correlation between prices charged and the depth of services provided is very evident here. The choice is yours—from red carpet service to "tie it down yourself." Both are courteous and helpful.

International Aviation, located south of the tower, is a first class facility. As you leave the taxiway, the golf cart with the "Follow Me" sign will lead you to their tie down area. Inside are two lounges decorated in Santa Fe style and a pilot lounge complete with DUATS. Thrifty Car Rental has an outlet in the building. At the time of this writing, fuel was $2.31 a gallon (100 LL). You will be asked to provide a credit card imprint before they fuel your plane. Tie downs are free and hangar space is generally available.
Phone: 505-471-2525

Zia Aviation, located at the north end of the ramp next to the Constellation, is primarily a flight instruction school. Mountain flying instruction, tail wheel and aerobatics instruction are offered. A full-time IA and a part-time avionics technician are available. A soaring school shares space in the office but is not part of Zia's operation. Fuel was $1.99 a gallon at the time of this writing. Tie downs are free.
Phone: 505-471-2700   Fax: 505-471-0905
Hours: Summer: 7 a.m. to 7 p.m. / Winter: 8 a.m. to 5 p.m.

Santa Fe Services

Chamber of Commerce: 800-777-2489
Ask for the *Visitors Guide* that contains an unbelievable amount of information. (Call the New Mexico State Department of Tourism for an equally informative publication that covers the entire state: 505-827-7400.)

Car Rentals: Most of the major national companies have offices in Santa Fe. Hertz, Thrifty and Avis (my favorite) have offices at the airport. Off field rentals can be inconvenient because the airport is miles from the downtown area.

Lodging: See the *Visitors Guide* for a complete listing. Santa Fe's main industry is tourism and the prices will <u>vary greatly</u> as the seasons change. Be very careful when making reservations and always get a conformation number. Competition is fierce and a budget conscious pilot can save a great deal of money by shopping carefully. At one motel, the price for a room for two people varies from $45 to $135 a night for the same room. Spring, early summer and late fall are the most economical times to visit Santa Fe. Avoid the last week of August and the first two weeks of September when Santa Fe hosts the Indian Market, the Spanish Market, and the famous Fiestas. Unless you like traffic and crowds, avoid the downtown motels and hotels. The majority of motels are located in the south side of town on Cerrillos Road (pronounced sir-ee-os). Santa Fe is a "city" and suffers the plight of escalating crime rates, so do not leave valuables in your car or take walks alone after dark.

The Santa Fe Trail Association

Many of the sites along the Trail and several sections of ruts that you will see are there because of the efforts of this organization. If you develop an interest in the Santa Fe Trail or in the history of the Southwest, consider joining this wonderful group of folks. Association members receive a quarterly newsletter that is packed full of information about activities, members and new publications relating to the Trail.

Formed in 1986, the 1300-member organization supports a variety of commemorative and educational activities throughout the year. Yearly membership fees of $15 (individual) and $20 (family) are worth every penny. If it were not for this dedicated group of people, many of the sites along the Trail would not exist today.

Santa Fe Trail Association:
Address:
      PO Box 31
      Woodston, Kansas 67675
Phone: 913-425-7312
Fax: 913-994-6255

Fantasy Fighters

If you have ever wanted to fly a Mig-15, a T-34 or a Yak-52, this is the place. Fantasy Fighters, owned and operated by Larry Salganek, is based at Zia Aviation. The aircraft are visible near the Constellation as you taxi to parking.

Larry offers a smorgasbord of training and flying experiences for pilots. This operation is not one of the air combat schools for pilots or non-pilots but a serious training organization. A two-day basic introduction to the T-34 and aerobatics consists of ground school and four hours of dual time in the aircraft. In those two days you will learn: aileron rolls, barrel rolls, slow rolls, loops, Cuban eights, splitS, reverse Cuban eights, hesitation rolls, Immelmans, snaps, hammerheads, spins, cloverleafs, avalanche and inverted flight. If that sounds like too much, Larry will modify the course to fit your needs.

Pilots that did not receive spin training in their primary instruction would be well advised to take advantage of this opportunity to become comfortable with spin recovery techniques. If you have not had much experience with high density altitude flying or need a high performance endorsement or BFR, the two day course can provide it all. (This is meant to be used as an argument to convince non-pilots in your crew to agree with your logical reasons to indulge in this fantasy.) Santa Fe offers almost endless diversions to occupy the time of the non-pilots during the two and a half days Larry suggests that you schedule for the course.

If you enjoy the rush of adrenaline, Fantasy Fighters offers the above course in a Yak-52 that will pull you through the sky behind a 360 hp radial. More power?? Other options and programs are offered in L-29 Delfin jets or Mig-15s that climb at 7500 feet per minute (sea level).

Larry has been an instructor for 20 years and has logged more time in military aircraft than in civilian aircraft. He holds Low Altitude Airshow Waivers in the T-34, Yak-52, L-29, and Mig-15. A busy schedule suggests that you call to arrange your fantasy as much ahead of your arrival date as possible. Larry can be reached at:

Fantasy Fighters
3662 Cerrillos Road, Suite A - 3
Santa Fe, New Mexico 87501
Phone: 505-471-4151
Fax: 505-471-6335

The Santa Fe Trail Association
Needs Your Help!

If you have been bitten by the "bug" and want to learn more about the Trail and its history, please contact the Santa Fe Trail Association and request a list of the books that they offer for sale. This list is the most comprehensive offering of Trail books that I have seen. Ordering books through the SFTA helps to fund and support this wonderful organization. Also, request a membership application.

When you join the SFTA you will receive a quarterly newsletter and other information listing events and happenings sponsored by the various chapters of the group. You will soon be convinced that the "Spirit of the Trail" is alive and well.

Contact the SFTA at:

Santa Fe Trail Association
 P.O. Box 31
 Woodston, Kansas 67675
Phone: 913-425-7312
Fax: 913-994-6255

Selected Reading

BEACHUM, LARRY M.
William Becknell, Father of the Santa Fe Trail.
El Paso, Texas: Texas Western Press, 1982.

GREGG, JOSIAH.
The Commerce of the Prairies.
Lincoln, Nebraska: University of Nebraska Press, 1967.

GREGG, KATE L. , ed
The Road to Santa Fe.
Albuquerque, New Mexico: University of New Mexico Press, 1952.

MACOFFIN, SUSAN.
Down the Santa Fe Trail and Into Mexico.
Lincoln, Nebraska: University of Nebraska Press, 1982.

RITTENHOUSE, JACK D.
Trail of Commerce and Conquest
Albuquerque, New Mexico: University of New Mexico Press, 1971.

RUSSELL, Mrs. HAL.
Land of Enchantment, Memoirs of Marian Russell Along the Santa Fe Trail.
Albuquerque, New Mexico: University of New Mexico Press, 1993.

SIMMONS, MARC.
Following the Santa Fe Trail.
Santa Fe, New Mexico: Ancient City Press, 1986.

(Note: Marc Simmons is considered to be the leading authority on the Trail and if you read only one book it should be his.)

Detailed maps:

FRANZWA, GREGORY M.
Maps of the Santa Fe Trail.
St. Louis, Missouri: The Patrice Press, 1989.

Photographing the Trail

About the Photographs in this Book
Without a doubt, photographing the waypoints was the most difficult part of preparing this book. Sacrificing the artistic freedom of
composition was necessary to capture an image that could be
recognized from up to 20 miles away. Many trips to Kansas were
made before the light and atmospheric conditions were suitable for
the camera. The drought in Oklahoma and eastern New Mexico in
1996 supported poor visibility from the dust. The photographs of
waypoints that were exposed from several miles lack some detail
but the images are clear enough to allow recognition.

A word of caution:
If you fly the Trail alone, the cockpit will become somewhat hectic
as you try to manage the controls and a camera or two. Please do
not neglect to avoid unscheduled contact with the ground or objects
attached to it. I came very close to an unscheduled landing on a
radio tower while trying to photograph a waypoint for my Oregon
Trail guidebook!

Tips for photographers:
Tape the focus to infinity and/or disable the auto focus if you have
one.

Shoot early when the light is low and the shadows are at their best.

Try to avoid shooting through plexiglass windows. Some auto-focus
cameras will see and focus on the plexiglass. If an open window is
not an option, try to keep the lens face perpendicular to the window
surface.

Underexpose the film and have the lab "push" it to increase the
contrast.

If you use the one hour labs, have your film developed each day so
that you can adjust your techniques if needed while you still have
the opportunity to reshoot if need be.

If you shoot black and white, consider using a yellow or red filter to increase contrast.

A haze filter will help clarify color shots.

The closer you are to your subject the clearer will be the image on the film. Take the time to position your aircraft for the shot. Do not try to shoot into the sun and keep the cabin shaded to avoid reflection on the inner surface of the windows.

Those of you who fly high wings be cautious of the underside of the wing. Not only will it pop up on the photos but the white under surface will mislead the light meter. Lift the wing and take a meter reading and <u>then</u> set the lens or shutter speed.

The appearance of the ruts will change quickly as the angle of the light changes. I have spotted ruts that disappeared 30 minutes later when I returned to photograph them. Again, early morning is the best time to shoot the wheel scars.

Film Speed: This is a tough one. For color work I have found that 100 works well. A little more latitude is provided by using 200 if it is not a bright day. For black and white, with up to a yellow filter, 100 will work if you slow the plane a little and isolate the camera from vibration. For a red filter, 400 is almost a necessity but plan on some grainy prints if you enlarge much.

Video: You are on your own. I have not tried it. I am told that the auto focus will sometimes focus on the plexiglass as it does in some still cameras.

If you end up with some good shots, send them to us with a description of the location and we will consider them for use in the next edition of this book.

Last but not last, shoot lots and lots of film. Shots from the air are tricky and the more exposures that you make the better are your chances of success.